DELIVERED
but <u>not</u> HEALED

DELIVERED
but not HEALED

Marcia Dixon-Haye

CONCLUSIO
HOUSE PUBLISHING

Copyright © 2015 by Marcia Dixon-Haye

All rights reserved. This book or any portion thereof may not be reproduced or used in any manner whatsoever without the express written permission of the publisher except for the use of brief quotations in a book review.

www.deliveredbutnothealed.com

Printed in Canada

First Printing, 2015

ISBN 978-0-9938420-7-8

Published by:
Conclusio House Publishing
10-8550 Torbram Rd.
Suite 430
Brampton, ON
L6T 0H7

www.conclusiohouse.com

Dedication

This book is dedicated to my loving husband, Lee-Roy, and my children, Kenesha and Anthony.

To my precious mother, Evangelist Linnette Lewis, who has always believed in me, and who keeps praying for me.

To my pastor, Bishop Thompson, and his family. To my church family and all my friends. To my father, my sisters, Elizabeth, Joan, Michelle, Carol, Ann-Marie, and my brothers, Delana, Rhue, Peter, and Gauntlet.

This book is also dedicated to all the women and men who are hurting and struggling to overcome childhood pain.

And finally, to all the survivors of childhood hurt who have been delivered and healed.

Acknowledgements

First and foremost, I'd like to thank my Lord and Saviour Jesus Christ for helping me to write this book.

Thank you to my husband, Lee-Roy, my two children, Anthony and Kenesha, and my wonderful mother, Evangelist Linnette Lewis, for all the love and joy they bring into my life.

Thank you to my bishop, pastor, and spiritual father and his family, and also my church family for supporting me tremendously. You have taught me so much about myself and about life. Thank you for helping to facilitate healing in my life.

Special thanks to Dr. Clarence Duff for helping to make this book possible. And thank you to Canada Christian College and all the staff.

Thank you to Women's College Hospital and the mental health and WRAP department for so graciously supporting and helping me to make this book a success.

Thank you to Sandra Bailey for her humility, love, devotion, encouragement. Thank you for your dedication and tremendous help in making this book a reality. You are an amazing young lady.

Thank you to the Mount Zion Apostolic Bible College, Dean Dr. Colin Cowley, and all the staff of the college. Thanks also to Kingdom Life Bible College, Dean and Pastor Dr. Barrington Smith, and all the staff.

And to all those who helped to process me, who stood against me in opposition and adversity, thank you so much. You have helped to push me onto the path of my ministry and destiny. Satan meant it for evil, but God meant it for good.

Table of Contents

Foreword by: Dr. Clarence Duff .... *xi*
Preface .... *xiii*

Introduction: The Battle for the Mind *1*
Chapter One: The Importance of the Familial Bond *4*
Chapter Two: The Home and Early Development *19*
Chapter Three: Understanding Abuse *37*
Chapter Four: The Hidden Pain *59*
Chapter Five: Dealing with Negative Emotions............... *69*
Chapter Six: The Nature of the Christian Conversion .. *82*
Chapter Seven: Redefining Your True Self *88*
Chapter Eight: The Making of a New Mind *100*
Chapter Nine: From Deliverance to True Healing *109*
Chapter Ten: From Ordinary to Extraordinary *120*

Conclusion *123*

Appendix: *124*
    Value I Cherished *125*
    The Creaking of the Door *127*

Bibliography *130*

Foreword

Some people are of the opinion that time heals. Others believe that becoming a born again believer immediately erases the pain and hurt of past experiences. However, more and more we are observing that time does not heal, and becoming a Christian does not suddenly resolve old wounds and erase hidden pains. It is no secret that long after becoming a Christian many continue to suffer from the effects of their past experiences of abuse. While it is true that healing occurs over time, time is never the instrument that brings about healing.

In *Delivered but not Healed,* Marcia Dixon-Haye brings us a refreshing and helpful understanding not only of the effects of past abuse, but also of the healing capacity of conversion, biblical instruction, and the fellowship of the church. Drawing on timeless instructions from the pages of Scripture, Marcia presents key principles for dealing with the hurt and pain from childhood experiences. She provides the reader with profound insights as well as practical tools for the journey towards healing, all the while giving careful attention to healing resources inside the individual and within the body of believers. Each chapter takes the reader into a deeper understanding of self, change, and healing.

I am thankful that Marcia has chosen to highlight some of the deep concerns that many within the church have been living with for years. For this reason, I recommend this book to all who are seeking to move beyond past debilitating experiences that have left them with emotional scars. I also recommend this book to all those who are concerned about helping people heal and become all that God intends for them to be.

Clarence Duff, Ph.D.

Preface

For years I wanted to write this book because of the many traumatic things I experienced in my life. As I reflected on the goodness of Jesus Christ and His awesome healing power in my life, I purposed in my heart that I would write to show that when Jesus said that by His stripes we are healed, He was not just talking about a physical healing. In truth, His stripes took care of our complete healing—emotionally, psychologically, spiritually, and physically. I once visited my professor's church and heard him preaching on the topic of deliverance and healing, which sparked a fire within me. I was stirred and, more than ever, encouraged to write for the sake of others who are trapped in similar situations.

The sermon was so profound that I could not get it out of my thoughts. As the pastor unravelled the truth of God's Word, I realized that although many people may be delivered from the situations and challenges they experienced, they still live with the pain and scars that have not healed. I had an immediate connection to the message because I have been through emotional trauma that almost left me dead, but God wrought a miraculous healing in my emotions, my body, and my spirit. Today, I am no longer a victim, but a victorious woman of God with potential and a successful future. My future is brighter than my past because of the healing power of Jesus Christ.

As the pastor explored the idea of being delivered (drawn out of a situation), but not healed, he used the example of a soldier who he is delivered from war, but who is left with post-traumatic stress disorder. During this sermon, I realized how my own emotions were tied up and how they affected all the areas of my life. We will be looking at these factors throughout the book as we explore the different ways in which we can be hurt. As I sat and listened, I realized that people's behaviour has a lot to do with what they have been through or what they are presently experiencing. People experience family crises, childhood pain, the pain of abandonment, shattered dreams, the pain of failure, rejection, abusive marriages, and disappointments.

During the sermon, I realized that most people don't need a medical doctor or money, but hope for these trying times. I hadn't realized the depths of the emotional scars I carried from my childhood, and the depths from which Jesus delivered and heal me. The picture of my past and the connection between the two were so vividly painted. And the beauty of it all was that I was able to sit through the sermon without feeling any kind of hurt or emotional pain, all because Jesus's delivering power had set me free and healed me.

This book is an attempt, through the power of the Holy Ghost, to uncover the mask of pain and the hidden scars. I believe that the time has come for us to tell people not what we know, but what they need. Normally, people who encounter these kinds of trauma are in need of hope, healing, and security. However, this can only be done through the process of releasing the persons who betrayed their trust, and seeking the path of healing. The second aim of this book is to show the power of the blood of Jesus Christ and the power of His Church. My third goal is to help victims bring closure to the past, break free from emotional pain, bring healing to their inner child, and move on to a bright and prosperous future.

For many, the abuse, neglect, and rejection might have just been for a moment, but to recover the emotional stability, self-confidence, and trust can take years. The healing process is a journey, but with the skillful hands of Jesus, this journey will be successful. As we journey through this book, you will find strength to bury your past, and you will experience the metamorphic experience of a caterpillar transforming into a butterfly. This transforming process will renew your mind and change your perspective of life.

In this book, we will revolutionize our lives, capture the things we lost, reprogram our thinking, and rediscover and redefine ourselves by breaking the bonds that hold our minds and emotions in captivity. In order to facilitate our healing, we must first change our mindsets and our words, and begin to speak prophetically over our lives according to the Word of God. Jeremiah 29:11 declares, "For I know the thoughts that I think towards you, said the Lord, thoughts of peace, and not of evil, to give you an expected end." God has validated us and has set us in heavenly places in Christ Jesus. Therefore, you no longer need to look for validation from man because the Lord has already validated you. We have the inner ability and the inner strength to recover all. We no longer have to succumb to the plot of the enemy to destroy our lives.

This book is about meaningful change, breaking bondages, dealing with feelings that are suppressed, hidden, or unacknowledged. In John 11 when Jesus called Lazarus from the grave, He told the people to loose him and let him go. Likewise, it is time to step out of those grave clothes. Luke 13 also tells of a woman who had a spirit of infirmity for eighteen years. She was confined in that situation and could not enjoy the stars and the view of the skies because she could not raise her head. She spent all her money going to physician after physician, until that day when she came in contact with Jesus. When Jesus showed up, all the powers of darkness were utterly destroyed. By the power of God, this woman was set free from the spirit that had held her captive for eighteen years.

Jesus Christ is the only physician you will come in contact with who will heal you spiritually and physically without you having to spend a dime. As we explore the topic of healing, you will see why you must fight for your life and free yourself from the plague of childhood trauma. It is time to stop the bleeding. It is time to stop the weeping. It is time to arise. Let the Deborah in you arise and take your place in the earth. It is time for you to rediscover your authentic design.

Marcia Dixon-Haye

Introduction
The Battle for the Mind

Our battle started in the Garden of Eden, where the enemy distorted the Word of God and influenced Eve to believe his manipulative lies. Our thinking influences our lives. Hence, the enemy tries to infiltrate our minds with negative thoughts and seeds of distorted perceptions. Eve had a choice. Her choice was influenced by her thoughts, and her thoughts were influenced by the deceptive words of the evil one. Yet, even though she was influenced, she had a chance to choose what God said over what the enemy said to her. Unfortunately, her choice has led to us having to engage in a battle of the mind today. Satan's vain thoughts and twisted words caused Eve to reproduce the negative and deceptive seed that negatively affected her life and all of ours today.

We face a continuous war that the enemy is waging for the souls of men and women. It is a war between the kingdom of darkness and the kingdom of God. It is said that in a war, a country can lose the battle, but win the war. However, on this unseen battlefield, we must win the battle in order to win the war, because if we lose the battle for our minds, we have lost the entire war.

Every day we wake up the battle is intensified, like a raging sea. The battle is over strongholds, it is over positive thoughts versus negative thoughts, and over the manipulative lies of the enemy. Some of these strongholds are influenced by our environment, the media, and our cultural beliefs. Some of the seeds the enemy plants are through toxic people—people who are very judgmental and critical, who have superstitious minds, and who believe that God is speaking to them when He is in no way communicating with them. In actuality, the enemy has deceived them, and they have fallen prey to his manipulative tricks.

Life has thrown some punches and darts at me, so I know what it's like to be bombarded with negative thoughts and wrong perceptions. My experiences shaped the way I thought for a long time. But then I felt this warrior spirit within me that was armed, dangerous, and ready to fight, one that would not back down from the opposing enemy. The battle for my mind was won over two thousand years ago by the great commander Jesus Christ. He is our battle axe, and He has equipped us with weapons of war to counteract the wiles of the enemy. At some point, we will have to be like Nehemiah who, when he was opposed and oppressed by the enemies around him, positioned his men to build with one hand and fight with the other.

In this war, we must use the shield of faith to quench all the fiery darts of the enemy. His darts include deception, lies, accusations, negative thoughts, twisted perceptions, depression, hurt, anger, fear, oppression, shame, and negative self-talk. Therefore, we must daily pull out our offensive weapons to tear down the strongholds that threaten to imprison our minds. We must use the sword of the spirit, which is the Word of the living God. The scheme of the enemy is to make us believe his lies, like he convinced Eve in the Garden of Eden, but our weapons are proficient, and we cannot go under when we use them. Today, Satan's strategies might be a little different, but his intentions are the same.

At one point, Saul tried to let David use his armour, but David, having been in battle before, knew he was already armed with the armour of God, and so refused to put on the armour that would cause him defeat. The battle we face is violent and relentless. It is an invisible war, but we are quite aware of the enemy's crafty devices. We must be equipped, dressed, and armed for this battle. In order to win, we must organize our thoughts, be careful of the things we perceive, and eliminate the toxic thoughts that come to pull us down.

What you think is who you become. What you think is what you will feel, and what you feel is the behaviour you will display. Fight to maintain your integrity. Fight to hold on to your lifeline, which is Jesus Christ. Fight to stay afloat, and fight to stay alive. Never give up. Don't lay dead to the enemy of your soul. It's time to fight for your mind.

Chapter 1

The Importance of the Familial Bond

The most important thing in this life is relationship. God takes the idea of relationship very seriously. When man fell in the Garden and lost relationship with Him, God gave His only begotten Son as a sacrificial offering to restore man's relationship with Him. In Genesis 3, the Bible tells us that God came down in the cool of the day to communicate with Adam. God established a foundation for His relationship with Adam. Likewise, relationships must be built on a solid foundation.

A relationship can only be valuable to a person when they have first built a relationship with themselves. Having a healthy relationship with yourself is something that will filter and flow through your life with everyone you come in contact with. It is necessary to practice loving yourself, paying attention to yourself, nurturing yourself, strengthening your weaknesses, treating yourself to the essential things in life, talking to yourself to cope in life's storms, taking time to understand who you are as a person, and valuing yourself. Doing these things sets the stage for building healthy and solid relationships with others. Life is about building and maintaining relationships. This is what God gave back to us through the sacrificial offering of his only Son, Jesus. The relationship built with oneself then stems to the family system that is attached. You must be able to transfer yourself in a family system.

When a relationship that is supposed to be filled with love and understanding is disfigured, the victim's self-image becomes damaged. A child that is raised in a broken home can feel as though his whole world is broken. The early years of a person's life can shape the rest of their life because it is during these tender, vulnerable years that their sense of security, self-worth, identity, trust, and confidence are instilled.

Relationship with God

God made us to be in relationship with Him. He is all about family relationships, our relationship with one another, and our relationship with Him. In Luke 10:27 we are instructed to "love the Lord thy God with all thy heart, and with all thy soul, and with all thy strength, and with all thy mind; and thy neighbour as thyself." And throughout the Bible we see where relationship is used to hold mankind together. Relationship causes people to be successful, to be healthy, and to have longevity.

Below we will look at how certain parental relationships affect us during our childhood.

Why a Father Matters

Job 33:4 declares, "The spirit of God hath made me, and the breath of the almighty hath given me life." It is not a coincidence that the Bible refers to God as our Father. A man who is a father, or one who is an acting father, plays a significant role in his child's development. Whether that father is present or absent in his child's life, he leaves a mark, be it emotional, social, or physical.

In many parts of the world, children are growing up without knowing what it is like to feel a father's love. And if a father's presence can have a positive influence on the development of a child, then a father's absence can have a negative effect. There is a void in every child's life that can only be filled by a father. Though a mother may nurture and care for her children, there are some things that only a father can provide for his child.

Fathers have the ability to give life to their children and to keep their human spirit alive by the moral support they give. A father holds things together physically, spiritually, socially, and intellectually. His unique strength and ability to build the home also instills a sense of security in his children. In reference to Jeremiah 31:29, Dr. Ditta M. Oliker, Ph.D. states, "this quote from the Bible represented the power of the father as the primary authority of the family for many centuries." [1] Dr. Oliker explains the influence that a father has on his children and his ability in that leadership role. We see here that

---

[1] "The Importance of Fathers." Psychology Today. https://www.psychologytoday.com/blog/the-long-reach-childhood/201106/the-importance-fathers. 15 May 2015.

fathers set the stage of stability and strength in their children. A father helps his child to feel emotionally secure and sets the stage for better social connections with friends, family, and the community. As such, children who grow up without a father, grow up with a missing link. Boys need their fathers to model and teach them how to be independent, how to be good providers, and how to care for their families. Girls need their fathers also, for different reasons.

A Father in His Son's Life

In a world where brokenness has shaped many children, the absence of a father—through neglect, divorce, or a traumatic event—can contribute negatively to a child's life. A father's absence can lead to dysfunctional behaviour, low self-worth, low-self-confidence, and other forms of emotional imbalance in a child's life.

When a father is present in his son's life, it can improve that child's development by building stability, self-esteem, and confidence. A father is a role model and a hero to his son. He is the foundation of his son's future and his instructor in becoming a man. The love, nurture, care, and respect that he shows will be embedded in his son's life forever. When a father engages in effective communication with his son, a strong bond and connection develops in their relationship. It is crucial for him to invest his time, energy, money, and godly qualities in his son's life. By doing so, his moral values will live on from generation to generation as his son emulates him.

I conducted an interview with a young father about fatherhood for this section of the book. The following are the questions asked and the responses given.

Interview

Q. As a father, what do you expect from your son and how have you communicated this to him?

R. All I need from my son is respect, and communicating this to my son was easy. I explained to him that showing respect is the result of true love, and that if he respects me as his father then he will obey me as my son. And when he obeys, the Bible says his days will be long and prosperous upon this earth.

Q. As a son, what did your father teach you about being a man?

R. One of the most important lessons my father taught me about becoming a man was with the proverb "One hand can't clap." What he meant was that when I become a man, it is necessary for me to find my help mate—my wife—and we should strive to do everything together.

Q. At what point in your life did your father have the most influence over you?

R. During high school. Although he wasn't around because of being in another country, he made sure I had everything to get me through each year of school for all five years.

Q. What has been the most challenging and rewarding part of being a father to your son?

R. The most challenging part of being a father to my son was trying to be the perfect father so that he wouldn't see my mistakes and be disappointed in me. The most rewarding was watching him excel in a gift he was born with—playing instruments.

Q. Describe your relationship with your father as an adult. How is it different from your relationship when you were a child/teen?

R. My relationship with my dad is perfect. He respects me and solicits my opinion for 95% of his decisions. This differs from when I was growing up, in that, I was more dependent on him at that time. I guess the saying is true, "Once a man, twice a child."

Sons rely on their fathers to demonstrate to them what it means to be a man. However, without a father figure present, a young man must rely on media, friends, and other external influences to fill this gap in his life.

A Father in His Daughter's Life

A father is the strength and backbone of his daughter. He is her first teacher and mentor. He is her confidante and her friend. He is the one who first teaches her how to trust and how to love both herself and others. Hence, she subconsciously places her faith in his influence, motivation, aspirations, strength, and courage. A father is a part of his daughter's early support system. So if he is an emotionally and spiritually grounded person, he can be his daughter's moral strength and compass, guiding her actions throughout her life.

In a healthy relationship, a young girl looks to her father for just about everything. As a wife looks to her husband to caress her and shower her with love, so does a little girl look to her father for love, care, and attention. When a father tells his daughter, "You are wonderful," and "You are beautiful," those words follow her throughout her life. Powerful words of affirmation and validation from a father to his daughter will serve as a foundation for her future relationships. Strong father-daughter relationships can only add to the relationship that a woman has with her partner.

It is a fact that in today's society many people grow up without a father and still manage to develop successful relationships. Nevertheless, the absence of a father can have a serious impact on how vulnerable and promiscuous his daughter becomes. Many fatherless girls tend to look for love throughout their lives, wanting to feel that fatherly affection and a sense of security. Many look for someone to trust and someone who will believe in them and validate them. Some even marry older men because of the void of not having a father.

As parents, we do not teach our girls to be vain, but we do teach them to believe in themselves and to trust their ability to accomplish anything they set their minds to do. Mothers have traditionally been seen as the nurturers and caregivers, but let us call fathers to a higher standard. This generation of tech-savvy, fashion-forward, socially-minded girls and women need fathers to give the emotional validation they are looking for, the validation that can sometimes only be satisfied by a strong male role model.

Precious Seed: It Starts In Childhood

Psalm 127:3-5 says, "Behold, children are a gift of the LORD, the fruit of the womb is a reward. Like arrows in the hand of a warrior, so are the children of one's youth. How blessed is the man whose quiver is full of them; they will not be ashamed when they speak with their enemies in the gate."

Children are precious seed. Throughout the Bible we see that God is interested in protecting the seed. Seeds have the capacity to reproduce and bring forth fruit in abundance. It is the infinite potential within the seed that our spiritual adversary seeks to destroy. God put within Adam the ability to be fruitful, to multiply, to fill the earth, and to subdue it. A seed also needs the proper soil type in order to grow and bring forth.

It is in Genesis 3 that we find the first account of Satan trying to destroy the relationship between God and humanity by convincing Eve to eat the forbidden fruit. God saw this and was determined that the second Adam would come through a woman and that the seed the woman produced would bruise the head of the serpent. Since then, Satan has made it his goal to destroy seeds. The Book of Exodus tells the story of Moses. Though she had two other children, Zipporah saw that her third child, Moses, was good. Moses was valuable to his parents to the extent that his mother hid him for three months from Pharaoh's soldiers who sought his life. Then, when it became increasingly difficult to hide him, she built him an ark of bulrushes and set him upon the river. Thus, Moses escaped death under Pharaoh's decree.

We too must place a high value on the lives of our children, whether we gave birth to them or not. Unfortunately, not everyone does. Some people do not have the desire to have children, and many who are physically able to have children try to limit the number they bear. Psalm 127:3-5 tells us that our children are our insurance policy, our secured investment. Happy are those who possess these sacred, valuable investments because they are a blessing. All aspects of God's creation were given authority to multiply and replenish the earth. God told Abraham that his seed would be great and, by faith, we are the seed of Abraham.

There is a wealth of potential locked up in every child, waiting to be released to grow in abundance. When a child is nurtured, loved, and encouraged, her potential will unfold. God places a special interest in children. He calls them a "reward and a blessing."[2] Hence, we can never know all that a child's future holds, and so must value every breath they take.

The psalmist recognized how precious and valuable he was to God and recorded it in Psalm 139:13-18.

"You are the one who created my innermost parts; you knit me together while I was still in my mother's womb. I give thanks to you that I was marvellously set apart. Your works are wonderful—I know that very well. My bones weren't hidden from you when I was being put together in a secret place, when I was being woven together in the deep parts of the earth. Your eyes saw my embryo, and on

---

[2] Psalm 127:3

your scroll every day was written that was being formed for me, before any one of them had yet happened. God, your plans are incomprehensible to me! Their total number is countless! If I tried to count them—they outnumber grains of sand! If I came to the very end—I'd still be with you."

Children should be our pride and joy, and treated as valuable resources since they are our future leaders, doctors, judges, lawyers, and the list is endless. As we empower them, build their character, and instill moral, positive behavioural dogma within them, their lives and futures are positively affected. For this reason, it is important that we raise our children in a healthy environment, with a healthy identity that will forever shape them throughout their lives. It is the early stages of development that determine a child's physical, emotional, and mental state. Their moral, cognitive, and social development are also hinged on what we do as parents. It is those moments that we spend with our children that will help them in life when they encounter adversity.

A Child's Self-Esteem

As parents, we need to ask ourselves this very important question: "How can I reinforce and establish positive self-esteem in my child?" Parents are children's first influencers. How a child evaluates himself—who he is, how valuable he is, and what he is capable of—depends on his parents' opinion of who he is. The word self-esteem refers to the respect or impression that one has of oneself. If an unhealthy image of that child is instilled in his mind, it will cause him to have a low self-esteem. We need to allow our children to be aware of who they are as well as their worthy qualities, and teach them to accept themselves as the beautiful masterpieces that God designed them to be.

It is one thing if a child is raised by a parent who has a low self-worth, but quite another thing when the child inherits the language and behaviours of that parent, leading the child to feel inadequate, insecure, and of no value to her family, school, or society. Jeremiah 31:29 states that "the fathers have eaten the sour grapes and the children's teeth are set on edge." In other words, whatever you release or portray will be the fuel you inject into your child.

Children need positive reinforcement in order to develop a positive view of themselves. A healthy self-esteem prevents them from being easily blown away by the challenges they encounter. Rather than being timid, they will be courageous and bold, having the resilience to withstand any kind of storm. Children see their parents as role models in both word and deed; they see the world through the lifestyle of their parents. In fact, the home is the first world children live in and come to embrace as their haven of success; it is the foundation that they will build their future on.

Along with being nurtured, cared for, and protected, children must be given the opportunity to express themselves when they are able to do so, as this will help them to develop self-confidence and better social skills than those children who are not given the same opportunity. Children whose expression is restrained tend to bring this sense of bondage into adulthood and become candidates for many psychological issues. Once upon a time, the idea that "children must be seen and not heard" was commonly rehearsed. But research has taught us that allowing children to articulate their thoughts and engage in dialogue is important to the development of their self-esteem. How can children feel that they matter and are valued if they are only given limited opportunities to share and contribute their thoughts? A parent who encourages his child to make choices and who acknowledges his child's accomplishments builds a healthy self-esteem in that child. On the other hand, a parent who undermines, belittles, and talks down to his child only contributes to the low self-esteem of that child.

Therefore, we must empower our children from the womb. We must endeavour to instill in them self-confidence, self-worth, and self-knowledge as we help them build strong characters, good morals, and positive dogma.

Valuing Children

When we value our children, they in turn learn to value themselves. It is imperative that a child knows her value and understands that her parents or guardians cherish and accept her. That child must be able to feel the warmth and care of her parents, guardians, or caregivers, for this produces confidence. And confident children become go-getters and great achievers. Hence, it is in a parent's best interest to nurture the healthy development of her child.

All of us have experienced some form of physical pain during our childhood. Some of us have fallen off our bikes, fallen off trees, or broken a hand or foot, but none of these pains is as devastating as the pain of childhood rejection by a parent. Every child needs to feel love and care, especially from their biological parents. Children need the support of both parents, with girls especially needing their father, from whom they seek support, protection, provision, and friendship.

According to Wikipedia, "the experience of rejection can lead to a number of adverse psychological consequences such as loneliness, low self-esteem, aggression, and depression. It can lead to feelings of insecurity and a heightened sensitivity to future rejections."[3] And according to Susan Anderson, "loving and wanting someone who does not love us back engenders a deep personal wound. Rejection hits a raw nerve whose root begins in childhood." To further elaborate on this point, she listed five stages of abandonment[4]:

1. **Shattering:** the devastating severing of the love-connection; shattering of hopes and dreams. The emotions experienced are shock, panic, despair, and feeling you can't live without your love.

2. **Withdrawal:** you're in painful withdrawal of love-loss, as intense as heroin withdrawal. The emotions are yearning, craving, obsessing, and longing for [that person's] return.

3. **Internalizing:** as you try to make sense of the rejection, you doubt and blame yourself. Idealizing

---

[3] "Social Rejection." Wikipedia. Wikimedia Foundation. Web. 15 May 2015.
[4] "S.W.I.R.L | The Five Stages of Abandonment | Susan Anderson | Abandonment Recovery." Abandonmentnet RSS. Web. 27 May 2015.

the abandoner at your own expense, narcissistic injury sets in and fear incubates.

4. **Rage:** reversing the rejection and having retaliator feelings. Directing anger towards friends who don't understand or are critical of the abandoner leads to more unhealthy actions.

5. **Lifting:** Rising out of despair, life begins to distract you. You begin to open up to love again and all its possibilities. You "swirl" through all the stages over and over until you emerge out of the end of the tunnel a changed person capable of greater love than before.

Unless you have gone through the experience of being rejected by someone who was supposed to care for and nurture you, you cannot fully understand the trauma and pain that children feel when they go through such an experience. However, you might have been judged or rejected by others, which then produced a hidden pain that causes you to react and behave the way you do. You may look for acceptance in every possible way. The hidden pain may cause you to be shy, sensitive, and over-protective of yourself. As a result, you may have felt misunderstood by someone from whom you expected a better understanding of your pain. Maybe you were married and experienced rejection from your spouse because he or she did not understand the hidden pain you carry. Perhaps you have internalized your rejection to the point where you lapse into periods of depression. We will further explore the effects of hidden pain in Chapter Four.

In order to increase a child's ability to flourish, the

following are needed:

- A home
- Stability
- The feeling that they are valued (by family, friends, social groups)

Many of today's youth are experiencing mental challenges; some cannot even stand to fail an exam or to be turned down from a job. They don't know how to handle failure, loss, or rejection. As such, parents have a great responsibility to teach their children how to cope when they experience traumatic events and challenges. Parents should build relationship with their children so that children feel comfortable approaching them and telling them the truth about their experiences. Parents can teach them how to vent in a safe environment and how to deal with bad experiences.

Children should be taught not to deny their feelings, but rather to express them and vent them in a healthy manner. They must be taught self-confidence and self-esteem so that when they experience pressure they will know how to cope and be resilient.

When children have an understanding of the importance of family and values, they will hold on to these fundamental values throughout their lives.

Chapter 2

The Home and Early Development

A home is a dwelling place used as a permanent or semi-permanent residence for an individual, family, household, or several families in a tribe. It is often a house, apartment, or other building, or alternatively a mobile home, houseboat, yacht or any other portable shelter[5]. The home is considered a place of refuge, it's a shelter from the turmoil and storms of life. It's where hope is cultivated

It is in the home that we share values and collaborate on all our dreams, aspirations, and desires for a successful future. It is in the home that we look for harmony, respect, love, support, trust, peace, security, safe refuge, and understanding. The home is a fortress, which means it is a place of refuge from danger. The home is also where

---

[5] "Home." Wikipedia. Wikimedia Foundation. Web. 10 May 2015.

children's fundamental needs are met by their parents or guardians.

The popular phrase "home is where the heart is" denotes that home is a place where one is content, where love abounds, and where we feel safe. If children cannot find security and stability at home, then it becomes a breeding ground for confusion, discontent, and disharmony. On the other hand, when the home is stable, children grow up with self-confidence and security.

A beautiful home is one that cherishes godly qualities, and is filled with warmth, care, and the desire to please God. When a household shares spiritual values, a solid foundation is established that is not easily shaken. Hence the phrase "the family that prays together, stays together."

The Importance of a Home

The Bible teaches that the family was designed and ordained by God. It was God who initiated the first family with the divine purpose and ability to be successful and fruitful, to procreate and fill the whole earth. The home is where we learn who we are, and it is where parents are given the responsibility to instill moral and godly qualities in their children[6].

Each family chooses its own way of developing and instilling values that reflect the principles of the family's leaders. Family dynamics have a lot to do with a child's behaviour because the experiences shared in the family shape a person's moral character. A strong family relationship is sacred and should not be tampered with.

---

[6] See Deuteronomy 6:6-7 and Proverbs 22:6

The family is the nucleus of strong schools, communities, and nations. A family's value system can either pull a family together or tear it apart[7]. By encouraging family togetherness, through prayer and positive interactions, parents and caregivers foster a supportive environment where children can seek help in times of trouble. The simple act of eating dinner together allows children and parents to come together and build bonds while communicating.

Stability in the Home

The word stability means the quality, state, or degree of being stable; as in the strength to stand or endure[8]. When a home is financially stable, socially stable, and emotionally stable it creates a healthy environment for both the children and the parents. Therefore, a stable environment should be the core of the home. It is important to note that certain changes in a family's dynamic can disrupt a child's life, and have either a positive or negative effect. After all, it is said that we are the product of our environment.

Nature versus Nurture

Over the years, there has always been a debate on the effect of nature versus nurture on a child's development. There are several controversial theories concerning which one has more impact on a child's development,

---

[7] See Ephesians 5:22-26; 6:4; 1 Timothy 5:8
[8] Home. Merriam-Webster. Web. 10 May 2015.

behaviour, and personality. From my perspective, both are important, as they both contribute in different ways to the child's outlook on life.

Psychology expert Kendra Cherry states:

Babies begin to take in sensory experiences from the world around them from the moment of birth, and the environment will continue to exert a powerful influence on behavior throughout life. Genetics can have a powerful influence on development, but experiences are equally important. For example, while the genetic code contains the information on how a child's brain may be pre-wired, it is learning and experience that will literally shape how that child's brain grows and develops.

While culture can play a major role in how a child is raised, it is still important to remember that it is the interaction of influences that dictates how a child develops. Genetics, environmental influences, parenting styles, friends, teachers, schools and the culture at large are just some of the major factors that combine in unique ways to determine how a child develops and the person they will one day become. [9]

Environment, parental influence, and genetics all contribute to the wellbeing of a child. Therefore, parents should do everything they can to provide a healthy and balanced life for their child. How children are raised has a lot to do with how they deal with the issues and challenges they face as they grow into adulthood.

---

[9]Cherry, Kendra. "Nature vs Nurture: Do enes Or Environment Matter More?" http://psychology.about.com/od/nindex/g/nature-nurture.htm. 09 May 2015.

The Family

Families are vitally important in this life; in fact, none of us can properly exist without a family. God established the family unit in the Garden of Eden, and so families are very important to Him. A child's identity and core values are formed in the family unit. A family with strong values, structure, and stability is able to fight back and survive crises.

With the uncertainties in the world today, it is of great importance that we focus on the family. Families should be our top priority according to God's design; that is why the church is the first family. The church has everything to offer to the community, and so God depends on the church family to carry out its sacred duties, which includes raising our children in the fear of God.

The family is responsible for developing healthy relationships that are cemented by acceptance and security. Parents are the cornerstone of the family unit and should ensure that they are available to build a "secure attachment" with their children. God uses the mother's bond with her child to demonstrate His love and attachment to us. If the bond is dysfunctional, it affects the child's personality. The healthy attachment of children to their parents is vital to their future attachment with their spouses and their own children. I'm in no way a perfect parent, but my own experience has taught me that a child needs to hone her individuality while balancing her attachment to her parents. It is not recommended that we become authoritarian parents who do not allow their children to reason or ask questions, and who constantly assert their authority over their children. But we can build strong relational bonds through a communication style that balances warmth, clarity, and firmness. The discipline and rules must create character and maturity in our children, not stress.

A high stress environment can trigger or activate vulnerability in children and change the chemicals in their brain. Some children tolerate and deal with stress better than others. While one child may be able to overcome setbacks, another might struggle to overcome his environment. Children differ and so will take different paths in life, even though they were taught the same core values within the home. Every child will deal with life's challenges differently.

Our journey through life is directed by various circumstances, such as abuse, rape, divorce, rejection, abandonment, and the list goes on and on. As our environment changes, we must keep in mind that we were created to shape our environment, and not the other way around. Both our genetic and environmental influences have a lot to do with our development, progress, and success in life. Therefore, our early experiences with positive influences make us stronger, more resilient individuals.

Yet early development is not the final stage in determining who we can become, in that, our past does not have to have the final say in regards to our future. The word of God gives us the internal resilience to move forward despite the circumstances we face. Change must first take place in the mind. God's word is so powerful that it can change the chemistry of our brains. That said, it is important not to focus on the pain or the past, for the deeper the despair the greater the success. In fact, your past has no power over you future. Oprah Winfrey, Joyce Myers, and Paula White are perfect examples of women who conquered adversity and went on to achieve great success. Their lives have inspired many of us to become comfortable in our own skin and achieve greatness.

Sibling Rivalry

Sibling rivalry is not a new concept and can be traced all the way back to Biblical times. Here are a few examples of sibling rivalry in the Bible:

- The death of Abel at the hands of his brother, Cain, was the first murder recorded in the Bible, and was an offence to God, to the first family, and to humanity in general.[10]

- While Rachel was pregnant with twins, the two brothers struggled within her womb. Even during their birth, the first of the twins, Esau, was born with his brother, Jacob, holding on to his heel. [11]

- Joseph was well-loved by his father, and this was seen by his other brothers. As a result, his brothers plotted to kill him, and later sold him to Ishmaelites. [12]

- When David was sent to the Israelite camp with provisions for his brothers, he was greeted with a reprimand by his brother, which suggests some hostility towards David. [13]

---

[10] Genesis 4:1-15
[11] Genesis 25:22-35
[12] Genesis 37:28
[13] 1 Samuel 17:28

Sibling rivalry is a type of competition or animosity among related or non-related siblings. The bond that usually exists between the siblings can be complicated and is influenced by a variety of factors, such as how parents treat each child, the birth order of the siblings, their individual personalities, or their experiences outside of the family. [14]

According to child psychologist Ho Sylvia Rimm, "sibling rivalry is particularly intense when children are very close in age and of the same gender, or where one child is intellectually gifted."[15] Every child is unique and so must not be compared to others, but instead should be viewed as an individual with an individual personality, and treated fairly.

Childhood sibling rivalry that extends into adulthood sibling rivalry causes relationship ties to be broken. According to Psychology Today, "while few adult siblings have severed their ties completely, approximately one third of them describe their relationship as rivalrous or distant. They don't get along with their sibling or have little in common, spend limited time together, and use words like 'competitive,' 'humiliating,' and 'hurtful' to depict their childhoods." [16]

According to the University of Michigan Health System, there are several factors that contribute to sibling rivalry. Children compete to define who they are as individuals. As they discover who they are, they try to

---

[14] "Sibling Rivalry." Wikipedia. Wikimedia Foundation. Web. 14 April 2015.
[15] ibid.
[16] "Adult Sibling Rivalry." Psychology Today. Web. 27 May 2015.

find their own talents, activities, and interests. They want to show that they are distinct from their siblings. Here are a just few causes or triggers for sibling rivalry: [17]

- Children feel they are getting unequal amounts of your attention, discipline, and responsiveness
- Children feel their relationship with their parents is threatened by the arrival of a new baby
- Children's developmental stages affect how mature they are and how well they can share your attention and get along with one another
- Children who are hungry, bored, or tired are more likely to become frustrated and start fights
- Children may not know positive ways of getting attention from a brother or sister, so they pick fights instead
- Family dynamics—for example, one child may remind a parent of a relative who was particularly difficult, and this may subconsciously influence how the parent treats that child.
- Children often fight more in families where parents think aggression and fighting between siblings is normal and is an acceptable way to resolve conflicts.
- Not having time to share regular, enjoyable family time together (like family meals) can increase the

---

[17] "University of Michigan Health System." Sibling Rivalry: Your Child. Web. 13 April 2015.

chances of children engaging in conflict

- Stress in the parents' lives can decrease the amount of time and attention parents give their children, which can increase sibling rivalry
- Stress in children's lives can shorten their fuses and decrease their ability to tolerate frustration, leading to more conflict.
- How parents treat their children and react to conflict can make a big difference in how well siblings get along.

Have you experienced any of these factors in your childhood that has caused you not to bond with your sibling(s)? Well, the time has come for complete healing and restoration in your family.

Sibling rivalry can be accentuated by parents if they are not mindful of their actions or choice of words. When children begin to perceive a difference in the way they are treated by their parents in comparison to their siblings, a seed is planted that parents need to be aware of. If left unaddressed, parents may unwittingly water this seed. On the flip side, some parents are conscious of the fact that they are treating one child more favourably than the other, yet continue to do so anyway.

Genesis 27 gives us the account of how Rebecca schemed with Jacob to take Esau's birthright. As the eldest son, Esau was supposed to receive the birthright, but with his mother's help, Esau's twin brother, Jacob, disguised himself and received Esau's blessing instead. As we read the account, we can almost hear Esau pleading with his father for one more blessing. When he realized that there was no more blessing for him, Esau lifted up his voice and wept. This was a heart-wrenching experience, all because of parental favouritism. When a child feels unloved or forsaken, that child will do anything to release his anger. For this reason, parents should strive never to show favouritism.

One has to wonder how Rebecca lived with this guilt. How could a mother hear her own son cry from the depths of his soul for a blessing, and still feel good about her actions? We also see in Genesis how Joseph's brothers plotted to kill him and eventually sold him to total strangers. His brothers mocked his gifting and called him a dreamer, all because their father, Jacob, demonstrated that he loved him more than his other sons.

In the New Testament, we see the same kind of rivalry between the prodigal son and his older brother. Jealousy set in when the prodigal returned home and was treated to a celebratory feast. Moreover, in a non-relational context, there was dissent between the Jewish and the Gentile Christian brethren in the New Testament church.[18] There is still fighting within families and within the church today. Sometimes it is because of favouritism, jealousy, greed, or covetousness. Hence, let us learn to accept that our children are unique individuals, and as such should be loved for who they are.

We are reminded in the Book of John that Jesus prayed for us that we might be one as He and the Father are one. It is possible for us to get along. It is possible for us to let go of the past hurts and pain that we carry

---

[18] See Galatians 2:11-19

for our siblings and Christian brethren. It is possible for us to rid ourselves of the jealousy, anger, resentment, guilt, grudges, accusations, and judgemental behaviour that we carry. We can do all these things by embracing the rich experience and the warmth of love that can flow between our hearts and our siblings' hearts. Doing so will cause us to communicate with a better understanding and have more meaningful relationships. The apostle Paul declared, *"When I was a child, I talked like a child, I thought like a child, I reasoned like a child. When I became a man, I put the ways of childhood behind me."*[19] Likewise, it is imperative that we accept each other for who we are and put personality conflicts aside.

The Black Sheep of the Family

If you have ever seen a large flock of sheep grazing in a field, you may have noticed that while many of the sheep are of the same colour, there is often a few sheep who do not look like the rest. These sheep are usually of a darker shade than the rest of the herd. These sheep are always outstanding and so are easily noticed. Similarly, a black sheep is "a member of a family or other group who is considered undesirable or disreputable; a person who is regarded as a disgrace or failure by his family or peer group; a person who causes shame or embarrassment because of deviation from the accepted standard of his or her group."[20]

Black sheep often view themselves as outsiders,

---

[19] 1 Corinthians 13:11

[20] The Free Dictionary by Farlex.

usually because they tend to be outspoken. Though they are members of the family, they have certain characteristics that make them stand out from the rest of the family. Are you always the topic at the family dining table? Do you consider yourself to be not as 'good' as the other siblings or as precious as your other family members? How has it affected your self-esteem and self-image? Are you ostracized by your parents, teachers, or peers? Has it lowered your confidence? Ask yourself whose report you are choosing to believe—is it that of your ostracizer, or is it God's? The Bible teaches that we are fearfully and wonderfully made. Just think of it, you are a survivor of the very things that could have destroyed you

The bitter roots that have been growing within you since childhood may be the cause of some of the challenges you have faced as an adult. According to Dr. Clarence Duff, "a great deal of who we are as adults, our responses to the external world, the kind of cognitions and emotions that dominate our daily experiences and the kind of perceptions we have of people, self and the world have some root in our early experiences as children."

By looking closely at God's word, you will gain important insights as it relates to who God says you are. Slowly, you will understand that a person's perception of

---

http://www.thefreedictionary.com/black+sheep. 15 March 2015.

[21] Duff, Clarence. Unlocking the Mystery of Depression: A Psycho-theological Exploration on How It Happens, How It Is Prevented, and How It Is Healed. Belleville, Ont.: Essence Pub., 2003. 186. Print.

who you are is not the reality. Knowing God's intentions for creating you the way you are can and will change your world. But in order to accept the reality of who God wants you to be, you must be willing to accept the changes that are necessary to get you to that place.

The Boy in the Man

We all encounter challenges in our childhood that cause us pain. This pain could be due to neglect, abandonment, rejection, or abuse—physical, emotional psychological, economical, sexual. Any of these experiences can leave a person traumatized. And the emotional pain is so real that it can be stored or suppressed in that individual's memory. Because it is locked in the memory, every now and then a person can begin to encounter an overwhelming feeling of emotion that brings the "inner child," who is in pain and in need of attention, to the surface.

There is a silent cry that emanates from this child whenever he encounters disappointment or rejection, a cry that is hard to ignore. It is this cry that has held him in transition. The loud screaming of the child over the years has caused the man to try to suppress it by becoming numb to the pain. But the cry of the inner child should not be misunderstood. It is not a cry of one begging to be nourished, but rather it is a cry for help. It is not a cry for deliverance from hardship, but rather it is a cry for permanent healing, peace, and joy.

The inner child wants freedom from pain, freedom from fear, and freedom from the monstrous memories that won't leave. This is the kind of freedom that the inner child is seeking. And he is depending on the man to find a way to bring release.

It is necessary that every man comes to grips with himself in order to put an end to the cycle that has been repeated, time and time again. All the energy that has been invested in this child must be released. He must release the toxins that are clogging his sense of direction, and he must detoxify his heart to avoid health complications. In doing so, he will develop a healthy identity—psychologically, mentally, and spiritually—that will help to steer his life in a positive and successful direction.

I became acquainted with an adult male who was molested by a family member when he was a young child. As an intelligent child, he was looking forward to a bright future. His dream was to be like his father, who was his mentor. His father was a respected community figure, who inspired his young son to believe that he, too, could scale the ladder of success. How unfortunate that such a life filled with promise would experience so many unexpected blows. Now, in his adult stage, he constantly revisits and relives his childhood pain. He has suffered feelings of loneliness, emptiness, anxiety, pain, and confusion that tormented him for years. However, he found it difficult to disclose his pain to others, and so allowed it to shape his life and alter his personality.

As he allowed the abuse to proliferate, his childhood laughter turned into bitterness. As a child he felt powerless and helpless. For years, in vain, he tried to understand the incident, but couldn't. Can you imagine the pain this child encountered as he suffered in silence? He also kept the identity of his abuser a secret out of the fear that others wouldn't believe him and that his abuser would retaliate.

He looked for acceptance and love from others, people he thought could help numb the pain and cover the secret he was carrying. Instead, he found himself the victim of abuse four more times by the various men from which he sought refuge.

As he grew up, he had no desire for the opposite sex. He felt vulnerable to men and guilty, as if he owed his life to them. As the years went by, he felt tormented. He sought happiness through his own family and friends. But as much as he sought their affection, he just could not embrace the love they showed him. He felt worthless and unclean, and contemplated suicide several times. He had girlfriends, but they never lasted. The volume of pain he held in his heart blocked him from receiving the love that was being offered to him. Unable to live a content life, this 'boy in the man' often stayed in bed crying.

He is now a middle-aged man who still lives like a young child. An experience from childhood has trapped him. As he shared his experiences with me, I could only remind him of a message I once preached, "Let the Child Go." He had to face his fears and take the death walk to slay the boy who was trapped within. In order for the man within him to live, he needed to face the pain he suffered. If you've encountered anything similar or close to this painful situation, continue to journey through this book, and you will find hope, strength, healing, and a new outlook on life.

The Girl Trapped in the Woman

From the day of her birth, she was her parents' pride and joy. She was a beautiful child—everyone said so. Her parents loved her, and she grew up in a good neighbourhood. Life should have been easy for her, but as she matured, she became a shy and introverted person. School became a challenge, since she could not concentrate on her assignments or even handle the structure of being in class. Being labelled as having attention deficit hyperactivity disorder (ADHD) got her professional help, but it wasn't enough.

Her physical beauty increased as she matured and she became very popular amongst the men. Throughout high school and university she had many boyfriends, but her relationships never lasted long, until she met 'the one.' After their marriage, things seemed great, but then, to the surprise of their friends, he filed for divorce. Today, she is single and filled with bitterness and resentment over her life.

As you read this account, you may be thinking, "How could this be? How could a young girl, who seemingly had a great family, become this shell of a person?" Only those who know the full story can understand. Behind the closed doors of her childhood home, this young girl was physically and sexually abused by the man who should have been her guardian and protector—her father. Her studies suffered, not as a result of ADHD, but as a result of not feeling safe at home. The constant worry about what each night would bring plagued her mind, leaving little mental acuity to retain school lessons.

As a result of the ongoing abuse, her perception of men was that they were figures who exercised control over her and who could inflict physical and psychological pain. But over the years, she learned to hide it. And she did. Though her body matured into adulthood, the little girl inside her remained the same. The little girl craved what all girls desire—the love and protection of a strong male figure. She used her beauty to her advantage and tried to seek out men to provide that loving father-daughter relationship she craved. Her relationships were lacking that je ne sais quoi, until 'the one' came along.

He was an educated young man who treated her well and loved her as only a man could, and the years of hiding her hurt and scars were over. But as much as she wanted to love and be loved, she found it difficult to love this man. Her insecurities that he would hurt her and misuse her became too much for him to handle. He was committed to the relationship, but she was unable to accept the love he was offering. A few years into the marriage, he realized that the issue she was facing was too deep for him to remedy alone. After begging for them to seek help, he did the only thing he could—he left.

Do you know this girl trapped in a woman's body? Do you know a beautiful woman who may have a bad attitude? Do you know a woman carrying years of pain and secret abuse? Do you know a woman who cries herself to sleep, yearning for a father, yearning for healing and happiness?

When you find her, hold her, and tell her that it is not too late. Healing is here. Life and love are possible when she deals with the little girl trapped inside the woman.

Chapter 3

Understanding Abuse

Abuse is defined as "a corrupt practice or custom, improper or excessive use or treatment, a deceitful act, deception, physical maltreatment."[22] Other definitions include misused power with the intent to manipulate or govern an individual in the name of love, trust, dependence, and confidence; with these in mind, the individual becomes vulnerable.

Abusers use their power to dictate the terms by which individuals should live. They use threats and fear tactics to manipulate and control others. This kind of false power can manifest itself as emotional, verbal, physical, sexual, financial, and spiritual abuse.

People from every walk of life experience abusive behaviour on a regular basis from family members,

---

[22] Abuse. Merriam-Webster. Web. 15 March 2015.

friends, peers, colleagues, and church leaders. Many of these forms of abuse take place in the home, the place that is supposed to be a safe haven. Unfortunately, for some, the home is a place where the most frightening abuses occur. As Dr. Clarence Duff explains in his book Unlocking the Mystery of Depression, it is in the home that we learn to be ourselves and to express our deepest fears and highest joy.[23] When parents misuse their God-given power to care, nurture, and protect their home, children suffer. Children who live in these kinds of environments begin to adapt and model the behaviour they see, thus continuing the cycle of abuse.

Many people forget why they are placed in a position of authority. It is a fact that children will look up to a teacher or an authority figure with respect and confidence. And when adults consistently interact with children in a friendly, respectful manner, it builds a sense of trust within the children, wherein they feel safe and valued. The moment an adult crosses the line by making unwelcomed advances, the trust that was built is immediately called into question.

We must all be aware of our God-given authority to teach our children in a godly manner, according to the laws of the country. "Child abuse and neglect have become priority issues at national, state, and local levels during the past two decades. As a result, an enormous amount of information is now available about child maltreatment. Several national agencies exist which are devoted to studying and increasing public awareness

---

[23] Duff, Clarence. Unlocking the Mystery of Depression. 26.

of issues surrounding child abuse and neglect, and several major universities have produced a huge body of research about the causes, effects and treatment of child abuse and neglect. Yet the problem is simply not being solved."[24] Based on their studies of child abuse, it is the contention of Iverson and Segal that those who inflict abuse on children are likely suffering from psychological problems of their own.

It is said that two to three million children are abused every year, and often, from their own parents. The past misconception about child abuse was that it was the result of strangers lurking around schools, or by members of the public, like a sports coach or a clergy member. The truth is that a significant number of abuse cases are perpetrated within the home by a close relative.

History of Child Abuse

Child abuse has existed for millennia, but because of the issue of definition, it has taken a long time for it to become a chief concern in society. The earliest clinical documentation of child abuse occurred in 1860, when French forensic physician Auguste Ambroise Tardieu published an exposé on battered children. He later published works on rape and childhood sexual abuse. At the time, he was denounced by his contemporaries for treating what was then considered discipline, a private

---

[24] Iverson, Timothy J. Child Abuse and Neglect: An Information and Reference Guide. New York: Garland Pub., 1990. 2. Print.
[25] Connelly, Elizabeth Russell. Child Abuse and Neglect: Examining the Psychological Components. Philadelphia: Chelsea House, 2000. 23. Print.

family matter, as child abuse. [25]

Ancient Times

The following excerpts describe the nature of child abuse in its most ancient forms:

> Child maltreatment, as we define it today, was at the time permissible behaviour. In ancient times, children were brought into the world to serve and carry on the family line. Infants were solely their parents' possessions and had no rights of their own. Consequently, the fate of a child depended entirely upon the needs and desires of the parents. Such a family structure was very conducive to maltreatment.[26]
>
> Ancient society also promoted maltreatment through its child labour practices with young children being subjected to harsh and demanding working conditions. For example, children as young as six years old were used as cheap labour, beaten, purposely malnourished, and subjected to unhealthy conditions, all in the name of employment. [27]
>
> Physical abuse and neglect, by our current definitions, were tolerated historically because these behaviours were often consistent with the needs of parents and society. Sexual abuse of children, other than incest, was tolerated for much the same reason.

---

[26] Radbill, Samuel X., and C. Henry Kempe. A History of Child Abuse and Infanticide. Chicago, Ill.: U of Chicago, 1968. Print.
[27] ibid.

Historically, children were 'loaned to guests' or hired out for sexual use. [28]

I cannot imagine what those children in ancient times underwent. Being loaned to a guest or hired out for sexual use is no less than cruel. Children who had promising futures were demeaned; they were not considered to be valuable. In some cultures, children were even sold into slavery to pay for the family's debt. Unfortunately, the trade and mistreatment of children for labour was not considered to be abuse.

In biblical times, the practice of child sacrifice was prevalent amongst certain cultures. This practice was sternly forbidden by the God of the Israelites. Leviticus 18:21, 2 Kings 23:10, and Jeremiah 32:35 all speak of the practice of offering children to the god Molech by passing them through a fire pit built to the idol. This practice grieved the heart of God.

Children are abused and neglected today by their parents and guardians for reasons such as financial burdens, stress, emotional pain, ignorance, and depression. Oftentimes, the perpetrators themselves were also victims of harsh circumstances like violence and abuse—sexual, verbal, and physical.

---

[28] Iverson, Timothy J. Child Abuse and Neglect: An Information and Reference Guide. 3. Print.

The Current Wave

Child abuse is still prevalent today in all its forms. In Canada alone, it is estimated that thirty percent of children are exposed to some form of abuse. [29] And globally, it is estimated that upwards of 275 million children are victims of child abuse.[30] Paedophilia and the child pornography industry have affected the lives of many children. Young girls and boys are sexually exploited for the sake of perverse pleasure. Furthermore, statistics show that this form of abuse affects children in both developing and developed countries. It is reported that the top five countries with the highest rates of child sexual abuse are South Africa, India, Zimbabwe, the United Kingdom, and the United States. [31]

In the June 22, 1984 issue of the Journal of the American Medical Association, Dr. Marilyn Heins of the University of Arizona (College of Medicine) grouped the factors that lead to child abuse into four categories:

1. Parents who are products of unhappy childhoods, who are often isolated, do not trust others, and have unrealistic expectations of children

2. A child who usually exhibits behaviour that

---

[29] "One-third of Canadians Have Suffered Child Abuse, Highest Rates in the Western Provinces, Study Says." National Post Onethird of Canadians Have Suffered Child Abuse Highest Rates in the Western Provinces Studysays Comments. Web. 5 Mar. 2015.

[30] "Facts on Child Abuse and Neglect - Canadian Red Cross." Red Cross Canada. Web. 27 Feb. 2015.

[31] "Child Sexual Abuse: Top 5 Countries With the Highest Rates." International Business Times RSS. 12 Feb. 2014. Web. 27 Feb. 2015.

causes a strong correction reaction from the parent (for example, an infant that cries continuously or an older child who is disobedient or talks back)

3. A stressful situation or incident that serves as a trigger. This trigger could be economic (e.g. job loss) or social (e.g. isolation from the community)

4. A culture in which corporal punishment is allowed or encouraged

Many people in our society associate the phrase child abuser with a person that is on drugs, a paedophile, or someone that is involved in pornography. However, child abuse occurs very frequently in the home, at the hands of family members or guardians. To many, this is far-fetched, but it is the sad truth.

Victims of child abuse often feel ashamed and sometimes believe that if they disclose the details of their abuse they will be accused of lying. Also, due to the trauma they've encountered, abuse victims often live in fear, and in some cases have been threatened. Many cases are overlooked because they are either condoned or covered up by family members who do not want to expose the abuser.

Why Do Parents Abuse Their Children?

This question has been asked repeatedly over the years. Yet the reasons why parents inflict pain on their children are so varied that it would be impossible to exhaust them all in this book. It is a fact that as we journey through life we will encounter various types of people who have experienced hurt and who do not know how to overcome that pain. Many have not even thought of the possibility of being healed, spiritually emotionally, or physically. And so it is said that "hurt people hurt people."

We hear of many situations in which parents intentionally or unintentionally neglect, abandon, or abuse their children. What I have realized over the years is that these parents themselves have encountered physical, psychological, and emotional pain, which sometimes result in them having a nervous breakdown. As a result of their own childhood trauma, some of these parents are dealing with all kinds of mental health challenges, such as compulsive disorders, depression, or other borderline personality disorders.

Another reason why parents neglect their children is the lack of understanding as it relates to the value and importance of children and how to nurture their development. Many have deprived their children of the basic essentials because they have encountered financial struggles, and as a result, some of those children end up turning to drug or alcohol addiction, have grown up with insecurity, feelings of anger and hate towards their parents. Some parents use their cultural values and rules to discipline their children, using forms of punishment that are more abusive than disciplinary. Depending on their cultural beliefs, people sometimes use the passage of scripture from the Bible that says, "He that spareth his rod hateth his son."[32] However, this verse is often used out of context. Yes, the Bible instructs us to discipline our children, but in a moderate manner. This form of discipline

---

[32] Proverbs 13:24

should not destroy the child, but rather it should bring correction. Growing up in the Caribbean islands, using the belt as a form of corporal punishment was a must and seemed to be the only means of correcting or punishing. Many who were raised in the Caribbean can attest that some of the discipline meted out by teachers, parents, or relatives was actually a form of abuse.

Some parents who had abusive parents may continue the cycle of abuse with their own children, not knowing any other parenting style. Another reality in today's society is that some parents are children themselves and, rather than focussing on parenting their children, they focus on recapturing their own lost youth, and they forget their responsibilities to their children.

Parents have direct control over their young children, and if they are not careful, they can (intentionally or unintentionally) inflict pain on their children. I have listened to the stories of many people from different walks of life, and there is one theme that is common in all cultures. Some parents are under so much stress that their children become their stress-release mechanism. The fact is that many people do not know how to cope with stress properly. Whether it is financial stress, the stress of caring for an extended family member, or having too many responsibilities, stress can leave people physically and emotionally drained.

In a time when the economy is failing, job loss and unemployment are on the rise, and people are more stressed than ever. Hence, financial stress and poverty are major factors in parental abuse.

Types of Abuse

There are various types of abuse throughout the world. Abuse can occur in every arena of life. You hear about it in the media and within your own social circles. It is scary to think about, but the reality is that most cases of abuse involve individuals who are closely related.

The following are some of the most common forms of abuse:

Verbal Abuse

Verbal abuse is a weapon used to cripple, destroy and distort a person's mental, emotional, and psychological growth. In elementary school, children used to chant, "Sticks and stones may break my bones, but words can never hurt me." This statement couldn't have been more false. In reality, words can sometimes hurt more than sticks and stones. Physical abuse hurts, and though the body has the capacity to heal itself, visible scars may appear once the healing is complete. But with verbal abuse, one does not always see the effects right away. Verbal abuse goes straight to the core of our thoughts and reason. Once uttered, the hurtful words reside in our thoughts and can be replayed twenty-four hours a day, seven days a week.

Have you ever been told by a parent that you would never amount to anything? Words that hurt and carry chronic wounds for a child sound like this: "You are no good," "You are worthless and will never amount to anything," "You are a mistake," or "I should have aborted you." This kind of verbal abuse can shatter a person's self-esteem and cause him or her to feel insecure and unwanted. Some people are bullied. They are called names, shouted at, and spoken to in an abusive manner. And if these actions are not reported, the teasing, blocking, blaming, accusing, judging, criticizing, trivializing, and undermining will continue. Some people were raised in a hostile environment that now influences how they communicate. As a result, they consider hurtful speech to be positive.

A person's speech reveals the condition of his heart because the Bible says that out of the contents of the heart the mouth speaks.[33] So the heart is as much of a problem as the mouth. Verbal abuse often comes in the form of bullying, which involves intimidation, threats, coercion, humiliation, trickery, aggression, mental mistreatment, and other tactics meant to psychologically destroy the victim.

Healing from verbal abuse is a lengthy process and can sometimes require various means of intervention. A simple "I'm sorry" will not suffice, as victims are usually disfigured mentally, emotionally, and spiritually.

Emotional Abuse

Emotional abuse is when an action or behaviour addressed towards someone is meant to devalue or demean that person. The Bible teaches us that we are very valuable to God. We are precious beings created by God's design and uniquely formed in His image. All humans can attest to this fact. We are indeed fearfully and wonderfully made.[34]

---

[33] See Luke 6:45; James 3:6
[34] Psalm 139:14

Therefore, when a person's sense of value is lowered, and they begin to think about themselves the same way their aggressor thinks about them, that victim feels denigrated. Labelling the victim as being crazy, summarizing their decisions as stupid, or telling them they are no good are all forms of emotional abuse. Even worse, this type of abuse tends to occur over a long period of time.

Controlling the victim's actions and thoughts by using false guilt to manipulate, or giving degrading looks that pierce the soul can cause immense emotional pain. Public humiliation and intimidation create fear and anxiety, causing the victim to feel uneasy. Other forms of emotional abuse include invasion of personal space, stalking, possessiveness, jealousy, belittling, isolation from friends and family, saying things like, "If you had listened, I would not have had to do what I did to you," and withholding sex or attention.

Emotional and psychological abuse are more dangerous to the victim than physical abuse because the intent is to destroy the victim from within. Emotional abuse sets out to interrupt the growth, success, and future goals of the victim. This kind of abuse is a very painful and traumatic experience, especially when it is done by parents or by someone who made a commitment to love and to cherish in the bonds of marriage. When this trust is violated, it shatters the victim's dreams, aspirations, interests, and focus.

When the abuser cannot have his or her way, that person may go as far as threatening to kill, to leave, to take away the children, to destroy the victim, the pets, or personal property, or to break or throw objects.

Emotional abusers use their power to devalue and make their victim feel ashamed, hopeless, and frustrated, hurt, and damaged. They repeatedly take advantage of the victim's vulnerability by using the silent treatment, brainwashing, mindgames, manipulation, or showing a lack of empathy towards the victim.

Everyone needs love and security. If these two things are absent, an individual is usually left with feelings of rejection, confusion, and worthlessness. And even after they have walked out of the relationship, the effects of the abuse can remain for years, preventing them from moving on. The Bible tells us that the Lord is near to the broken-hearted and saves the contrite in spirit.[35] Therefore, as abuse escalates, let us strive not only to rescue the victims, but to also heal them.

Physical Abuse

Physical abuse is the easiest of the various kinds of abuse to identify. It involves inflicting pain, injury, and harm to a victim's body. Physical abuse may consist of, but is not limited to:

- Biting
- Burning
- Choking
- Cutting
- Grabbing
- Hitting
- Kicking
- Pinching
- Pulling
- Pushing
- Scratching
- Shoving
- Strangling
- Tripping

---

[35] Psalm 34:17-19

Any of these actions as well as the injuries that result must be taken very seriously. This kind of abuse can result in death if it is not addressed in time.

Child Sexual Abuse

Child sexual abuse involves physical, psychological, and emotional manipulation and mistreatment for the sake of sexual pleasure. Specific examples of sexual abuse may include:

- An adolescent or adult physically forcing themselves onto a child
- An adolescent or adult exposing their genitals to a child
- An adolescent or adult fondling a child's genitals
- An adolescent or adult looking at a child in a provocative sexual lustful manner
- An adolescent or adult watching pornography with a child
- An adolescent or adult giving a child tokens, like money or gifts in exchange for sex, rape, sexual torture, or coercion into painful sexual activity
- Parents who have incestuous (sexual) relationship with their children.

Kenneth M. Adams, Ph.D., author of *Silently Seduced: When Parents Make Their Children Partners,* states that "Children are not property. They feel terrified and degraded when a parent, or any adult, is sexual with them. Cooperation does not equal enjoyment. They are too scared, too emotionally needy, or too starved for affection to say no."[36] He further states that "the child's core needs are rejected, not served. The child feels like an object, not a person. The real needs for love, nurturing, security, and trust are never met. Worse yet, the child is made to believe those needs are met."[37]

Immediate reactions to sexual abuse include shock, fear, and disbelief. Long-term symptoms include anxiety, fear, or post-traumatic stress disorder. This kind of abuse is very frightening and disturbs the physiological and emotional well-being of a person. Many children have lost their sense of stability, trust, direction, and purpose in life on account of these traumatic experiences.

There are many disturbed people in our society, who have been sexually abused and who now have distorted behaviours. Several people have shared their stories with me of being sexually abused by parents, neighbours, siblings, relatives, or strangers. The pain, fear, shame, and disappointment can usually be seen in their eyes. So young, so vulnerable, so trusting, so innocent, yet their trust is shattered by people they are close to or by people they have never met before. Most victims are left dealing with feelings that terrorize and haunt them for many years, and for some those feelings follow them into adulthood.

---

[36] Adams, Kenneth M. "Overt Incest." Silently Seduced: When Parents Make Their Children Partners : Understanding Covert Incest. Deerfield Beach, Fla.: Health Communications, 1991. 11. Print.
[37] Ibid. pg 57

If the victim is an introvert, the abuse will take a toll on her physically and emotionally as she suppresses and internalizes these traumatic events. As the wounds get deeper and as they are suppressed and denied, she may experience memory lapses. Those who are extroverted will probably become defensive and protective of their personal space. These children sometimes become overly sensitive. Therefore, when counselling these individuals, one must be very careful of word choice, since words can be triggers, and the individual may begin to relive the experiences.

Not only do these children suffer from hidden pain due to trauma, but some also suffer from the threats made by their abuser. Many live with fear and suffer from panic attacks, not knowing when or if these threats will actually be carried out. These traumatic experiences have caused many to lose their true identity and develop feelings of insecurity, worthlessness, and incompetence. They will often try to overcome these feelings by striving to emulate the success of others. Many struggle with validation. It doesn't matter how well they do, they have difficulty feeling good about themselves without someone else validating them. They also frequently compare themselves to others. They struggle to see their own strengths.

Many people are unaware of the devastating effects that sexual abuse has on children and how it can define them in adulthood. Many husbands and many wives have suffered because of their lack of understanding as it relates to their spouse's behaviours, especially if their spouse failed to disclose the pain they endured in childhood

The influence these experiences have on a person can shape his or her life. Some have used these experiences to climb the cooperate ladder of success and have refused to let their past define them. But others have been held down because of their inability to get beyond their past.

Financial Abuse

If you're in a relationship and your partner seriously controls or restricts your access to money, then you may be the victim of financial abuse. The following are some of the techniques used by financial abusers:

- Refusing to give money
- Limiting the amount of money one is given over a period of time
- Demanding an account for all the money one has and spends
- Denying one access to bank accounts (via bank cards, credit cards, cheques)
- Preventing one from having a job (bringing about financial dependence on the abuser)

If a person of trust takes money earmarked to a child and spends the funds unbeknownst to the child, this is also classified as financial abuse.

Relationship Abuse

A relationship is an emotional attachment between individuals. As we go through life, it is inevitable that we will be required to build relationships. Relationships have different meanings to different people. Some relationships are platonic—intimate and friendly, without sex. Some relationships are work-related and exist only within the work environment. Other relationships may be spiritual, involving a connection that extends beyond the body. Unfortunately, relationships can also be superficial (not based on a firm foundation), one-sided (one party reaps all the benefits), or toxic (one party is constantly being hurt). Relationships play a very vital role in our lives; therefore, we must endeavour to build good, healthy, solid relationships that are long-lasting.

A relationship between two consenting parties established on mutually agreed-upon terms and expectations is likely to stimulate a healthy environment that is ideal for the wholesome upbringing of children. We want children to grow up with a good attitude, a good sense of direction, and with the capability to live a morally good life. It is said that children live what they learn.

Building a healthy relationship from the onset is vitally important to the outcome. The key elements for building are love, trust, sincerity, respect, and appreciation. Each person must try to understand the other's likes and dislikes, be open to change and adjustment, must support the other, agree to disagree without animosity, be a good listener, think before speaking, accept differences and the other person's rights, criticize in a constructive manner rather than a destructive one, and try not to be judgmental.

In some relationships, one person can exert so much control over the other that this person can eventually develop into an abuser. How could the person who is supposed to love and appreciate you become like a vampire that sucks the very life from you, depleting all your energy? This behaviour may be subtle and hard to recognize at first, until you begin to lose confidence in yourself and start to experience feelings of confusion, anger, depression, frustration, hopelessness, and loss of control as a result of the abuse you've suffered.

An abusive person may be a bully outwardly, but inwardly he or she may be a highly insecure person. Many abusers have been through traumatic childhood experiences or have grown up in dysfunctional families. Some have lost financial battles, and so they treat those with less power in an abusive and controlling manner in order to feel powerful and strong. But on the inside they are dying from an inferiority complex. They themselves feel a sense of worthlessness and find it hard to cope with how life has treated them. If you are in a relationship with a person who is controlling, be wary, this could become an abusive relationship.

Dating Abuse

Dating abuse is no different from marital abuse. It stems from the same kind of controlling, manipulative power struggle and behaviour meant to control, demean, and intimidate while rendering the victim powerless. Dating abuse occurs when one person controls the relationship. The abusive partner will often use guilt trips to get their way. For example, they will say things like, "If you love me, you will allow me to do this or that." Be alert, as these signs of abuse will escalate as time goes by.

Spiritual Abuse

Spiritual abuse takes place when one partner prevents the other from practicing their religion. It occurs when one demeans the other's religious beliefs. It can also be the reverse, when one partner tries to force their spiritual beliefs on the other.

An unexplored form of spiritual abuse is perpetuated by spiritual leaders and their affiliates. This includes, but is not limited to:

- Publicly shaming members for things mentioned during confessions
- Soliciting finances using scriptural references for alternate reasons
- Making sexual advances and forcing members to keep quiet

The Effects of Abuse

Abuse occurs in homes, churches, community spaces, at work, school, and even on public transit. The effects of abuse can be devastating and complex, depending on the kind of abuse. There are some victims who have completely lost their trust in other people, especially in the gender that abused them. These individuals often have a level of low self-esteem, feel dirty, unattractive, feel worthless, feel vulnerable, and feel unwanted and unloved. Most times they become easily depressed and tend to lose their confidence and self-worth just as easily. These people sometimes lose their sense of identity and, as a result, become confused in regards to their gender.

Some embark on a journey to find themselves, or to find happiness and a sense of belonging.

Even though they are not responsible for what happened to them, they are still plagued by guilt and shame throughout their lives. Their social lives become affected, and they become loners, having feelings of insecurity. Abuse affects how victims feel, think, and behave; it affects their social lives and even their spirituality. Some victims become abusive themselves; some become sexually promiscuous, and engage in substance abuse; and others struggle with anxiety and trust.

In a spiritual context, some become angry at God for not being there for them or protecting them while they suffered the cruelty of their abusers. On the other hand, there are those who find God to be the only father that they can trust, a father who sees all their wounds and heals their hidden pain. Despite the trauma, however, there are those victims who pull themselves together and manage to move on with their lives.

Many victims feel unworthy of love and that they will never be truly loved by anyone. The terrorizing memories of the past abuse haunt them and leave them with overwhelming feelings of shame, guilt, and self-blame. These effects cause many to engage in self-harm—inflicting physical injuries upon themselves—because of a false sense of guilt and built-up anger.

The primary responsibility of parents is to take the best care of their child by meeting their physical, emotional, developmental, and spiritual needs. Parents are given the authority by God to raise their children, and this authority is not to be taken as an opportunity to exercise lordship over them. Parents or guardians should never use their children as mates or partners. Children are God's gift to men and women. They are innocent, vulnerable, precious ones who depend on their parents and guardians for security and protection. When the parent-child relationship crosses the line to resemble a relationship entered into by two consenting adults, the consequences can last a lifetime.

Our children are a heritage, they are precious and costly, their future is bright and full of success. Parents should see to it that their children are taken care of, so they in turn will grow to take care of them. I am of the opinion that many children are behind bars, or become prostitutes or drug dealers on account of childhood trauma and pain.

As we move into the next chapter, we will learn how to conquer the enemy within and remove the limits caused by untreated trauma.

Chapter 4

The Hidden Pain

Life is filled with unwanted tragedy that can define our whole lives. Many terrible things happen to us in life, things that are sometimes too painful to communicate. I cannot get over the story of the secret pain in a particular royal family. David, the man after God's own heart, had a life that was filled with secret pain. God told David that the sword would not leave his family. In other words, David caused his family to come under a curse because of his decision.

2 Samuel 13 speaks of David's daughter, Tamar, who was raped by her half-brother Amnon. The Bible says that Amnon became sick for his sister; his countenance fell until it was noticeable. The devil had put out a decree and had marked the young girl's life, like he has done to many today. When Amnon was at his lowest point, the devil sent an uninvited guest into his life with cunning and crafty advice.

Amnon was David's first child, and a spoilt manipulating son, so everything he wanted he got. And so he asked his father to send his sister to make him a meal because he was feeling sick. We can agree that he was indeed sick, mentally, for only a mentally ill person could desire to strip his younger sister of her virginity, which meant so much to her. Amnon deceitfully carried out the advice and plot of Satan to destroy this young girl's life. Tamar, an innocent young girl with a bright future ahead of her, was disfigured and filled with shame. Out of her loyalty to her father, she was deceived and stripped of her dignity. That which was so valuable to her was taken away by her own brother. Tamar was left to bear the secret pain of the family.

The Bible declares that when David heard of the incident, he became angry. But God had told David that the sword would not leave his house on account of what he did to Uriah by sleeping with his wife, Bathsheba. David's immorality was handed down to his sons. The Bible tells us that David did nothing about the situation. Therefore, Tamar had to suffer the secret pain because of David's love for his first- born son.

Tamar then sought consolation from her brother, Absalom, but she went to the wrong source for help because Absalom was filled with jealousy and insecurity. He was very competitive, so the fact that David loved Amnon more than all his children did not rest well with Absalom. As a result he had carried a grudge in his heart against Amnon for years. Absalom was willing to try anything to make sure Amnon did not get to the throne. Therefore, when he heard what Amnon did to Tamar, it stirred up old the grudge and sharpened his desire to hurt him. The Bible tells us that he begun to hate Amnon.

Absalom could not foster healing for his sister

because he was broken and needed help himself. His anger accelerated from day to day, and he was filled with rage, bitterness, and vengeance. How could he foster her healing and bring her to a place of forgiveness, when he himself needed help? He needed to be delivered and healed from his own pain. David covered up the actions of his son at the expense of his daughter's oozing pain. She was filled with shame and unresolved pain.

Let us look at the scenario again. This innocent young girl was raped (sexually abused), then abandoned and neglected by her own father and the brother that raped her. This poor girl was marred for life. She was scared for life. Many of you reading this book have experienced similar things in your life during your childhood. Now you may be married to someone who does not understand your behaviour and your unresolved issues. It is time to remove the social mask you've worn for years, protecting and guarding your family's secret pain, while you are dying inside. It is your time of healing. Can you find the courage to heal? Can you find the courage to release yourself? It is time to pull out that inner resilience and fight back for your life. Your freedom is your choice.

Marital Breakdown

The break down in marriage has been the old traditional story that has haunted many marriages throughout the years. The worst problem you can have in a marriage is past hurts that have not been dealt with and that gradually eat away at the victim and spill over into the marriage. When people get hurt, undermined, abused, rejected, or abandoned in their past relationships, those hurts can fester over the years and shatter marriages. In marital relationships we should be open and honest with each other as we become one. Don't pretend all is well when you are really dying on the inside. Many hide their issues out of fear that exposing themselves to their partner will bring rejection. I believe that pastors and counsellors should ensure that they ask questions in premarital counselling that lead to uncovering past hurts and unresolved issues that could affect the marriage.

Communication is also a major cause for breakdown in families. Communication means to transit your thoughts, ideas, and any kind of information with clarity, whether verbal or nonverbal. Our attitude is important when communicating, that includes our posture, facial expression, and tone of voice. A healthy and open communication style sets the pace for resolving or dealing with past experiences and future goals and expectations. Healthy communication requires paying attention, listening, not being quick to speak, being mindful of body language, being comfortable in your own skin and with your partner.

I was once told by a mand that his wife would spend long hours on the phone talking to her friends, but would speak to him less than four times for the day. Another situation that was brought to my attention was of a man who only communicated to his wife when he wanted to be intimate or when it was money related. Otherwise, they would never have a healthy conversation.

The other cause for breakdown is money. This is a big reason for separation in marriages. "Your money is yours and mine is mine," is the motto that many partners use in their marriage. Some are spenders, while some are drifters.

The other issue is sex, which is a problem both in the church and in the secular world. All these issues break down marriages, and some are more severe in certain relationships than others. And if unresolved, these issues will only fester and cause marital split and pain for the children.

Choose to believe that no matter how bad the situation gets, how deep the wounds are, or how much effect it had on the family and on your life, there is still room for forgiveness. Lives do not have to be shattered, and children do not have to pay the price for senseless decisions made because of unresolved issues.

Hidden Pain

What is pain? Pain can be defined in several ways, but it is usually understood as a feeling of discomfort caused by an injury, disease, catastrophe, or anything that causes suffering, physically, mentally, or emotionally. In the field of social and personality psychology, the term social pain refers to psychological pain caused by harm or anything that threatens a person's social well-being. This includes things like shame and the loss of a loved one. Pain has the potential to interrupt one's day-to-day life and hinder one's aspirations. Physical manifestations of pain include a rise in blood pressure and irregular sleeping patters. Pain can also affect your capacity to learn and recall that which you have learnt.

Trauma is the emotional response that takes place after an unpleasant or tragic event occurs. Immediately after the event, a person typically experiences shock and denial. Even long after the event, the individual may still experience a range of reactions, from flashbacks to difficulty managing their emotions and the inability to move on with everyday life.

The autonomic nervous system controls all the other systems of the body, including the cardiovascular system, digestive system, respiratory system, nervous system, and muscular system. The brain contains the limbic system, which regulates the memory and the emotions responsible for pain and pleasure. This system contains the thalamus, and under the thalamus is the hypothalamus, which controls the autonomic nervous system. The amygdala, the hippocampus, and the hypothalamus all work together to control the emotional responses of pain, pleasure, and short- and long-term memory.

Melissa Healy wrote an article for The Los Angeles Times in which she mentions the brain's pain network.[38] The emotional ups and downs we encounter stretches across all cultures, and many people talk about the sting of social rejection as if it were a physical pain. For example, we feel "burdened" by a partner's infidelity, "wounded" by a friend's harsh words, and "crushed" when a loved one fails us. It's hard to imagine that we can go through these emotional pains and not be affected physically.

Eyes are said to be the windows to the soul. They can be filled with the fire of anguish and the pain of questions

---

[38] Healy, Melissa. "Heartache or Headache, Pain Process Is Similar, Studies Find." Los Angeles Times. Los Angeles Times, 4 Apr. 2011. Web. 28 March 2015.

left unanswered. Pain drains the human soul. And like the leech that sucks the blood of the living thing it attaches itself to, hidden pain has the ability to drain a person's emotional energy, changing the quality of life of its victim.

Pain is so unwanted that people have found different methods of dealing with its presence. Some use substances to dull the pain, while others wear masks to hide it. Some wear a smile in public, saying that all is fine, when in truth they have already sunken into despair and possibly depression. Both methods may offer temporary relief, but if left untreated and unresolved, the situation will become more chronic.

The Origin of the Pain

Emotional and physical pain that begin in childhood usually stem from parents who often fought each other, had financial difficulties, were incompetent, had over-scheduled lives, were neglectful, or were angry towards their children because of their own pain and disappointments in life. Many adults still struggle with the pain they endured in their childhood. Other traumatic experiences suffered early in life, like the loss of a loved one or rejection, can lead to issues later on in their adult life.[39]

---

[39] Collins, Gary R. Christian Counselling. Rev. and Expanded ed. Vol. 3rd. Milton Keynes: Word, 1989. 221. Print.

Power Over the Inner Child

Your inner child is the part of you that carries the memories of the traumatic experiences you encountered in your childhood. In Chapter Two, we looked at the inner child as it relates to "the girl in the woman" and "the boy in the man." Many adults have yet to come face to face with their childhood pain. They have abandoned, neglected, and covered up certain memories, but every so often they are plagued by these emotional wounds. Because they have not dealt with the issues, they now suffer from what I call "self-bondage," which hinders their relationship with others, impedes goals, dreams, happiness, and their ability to trust, love, and forgive others.

Ignoring or covering up your past is not the way to go. Neglecting the issue is never the answer, as it does not solve the problem. The best thing one can do is bring healing to your inner child's wounds by accepting those things in the past that you cannot change. Dealing with your inner child will help you to have a better understanding of yourself. Coming to grips and addressing those internal wounds will unlock the prison you have been caged in since the incident occurred.

One of the things that most therapists will tell you to do is to grieve. I, personally, constantly grieve for my innocence and bring it before God. Years ago, I took control over the wounded inner child that did not want to let go of the past hurt. I began to accept the reality of what I had been through and decided to face the shame and the pain. As I became an adult, I determined in my heart that my past would not imprison me any longer. I had had enough. I refused to let my childhood pain govern my life, so I came to grips with my past pain and compared it to my future gain. Doing so helped me to release the built up emotional pain, anger, and fear that I had been carrying. This was a conscious decision that I had to make in order to start building and maintaining relationships and a healthy lifestyle.

When I started to love my wounded inner child and accept my scars and pain, it became easier for my inner child to cooperate with the grieving and healing processes. I began to utilize my God-given power to control my surroundings and the rest of my life. One of the things I began to realize was the fact that I could look at another child having a similar experience and empathize with him or her. This was because I had been there. I began to assess the situation and ask myself why I couldn't feel that way towards my inner child, rather than ignoring the pain I felt. I realized that I had to embrace my experiences and weep, grieve, and release all the pent-up anger and frustration that I had in order to bring healing to this part of myself.

Many people's way of dealing with their negative experiences is to say, "Oh, it's in the past." Unfortunately, they have chosen to ignore the pain and, in so doing, they sometimes display behaviours and attitudes that indicate that there is a little child on the inside crying out for healing. This child can be triggered by the slightest thing that resembles the particular experience they had, and it sends signals to the emotional memory, causing the pain to resurface. Many adults are still running away from the things they encountered. They keep silent when they are hurting, and master the art of wearing a mask and hiding their true pain in silence.

There were days when I had to write myself letters

and journal about my childhood wounds and shame. I did that frequently until I got acquainted with my inner child. I soon understood what I needed to do to help this wounded child recover. It was through these steps that I was able to come to the point of conscious decision-making and let go, forgive, and allow God to release his healing power. Hating yourself will not heal you. Feeling guilt for what happened does not help. However, having a deep desire to be healed is the first step. As I began to open up myself to the Lord Jesus Christ and allow Him to cleanse and heal my wounds like the Good Samaritan who rescued the nearly dead man on the Jericho road, I no longer wanted my inner child to imprison me and prevent me from accessing the true potential within me. The moment I made that decision, my life, which was going downhill, took a turn for the better.

Today, I am no longer controlled by the wounds of my past. I am empowered and inspired by the power of the Holy Spirit to help others find their path to healing and discover their God-given purpose. I have discovered the joy of trusting in Jesus. No longer does my inner child dictate how I live my life.

Chapter 5

Dealing with Negative Emotions

The fact that we are made up of psychological, physical, emotional, and spiritual characteristics that are intertwined means that even after a negative experience has ended there are still psychological and emotional effects that remain. Many people across the world suffer from a condition known as post traumatic stress disorder (PTSD). It is a disorder that affects the brain and the memory. Traumatic experiences leave psychological scars on the brain, and sometimes people who have been abused report that they have no memory of what happened to them. This loss of memory is usually because the emotional pain has affected the hippocampus in the brain, which governs the ability to learn and control the memory.

Maia Szalavitz, neurologist and author of Born for Love: Why Empathy is Essential and Endangered, says in an article on health and family that, "Brains, like muscles, develop through use so regions that have been 'exercised' more tend to be bigger. But, abuse can interfere with development. To cope with overwhelming experiences of distress, the brain can alter patterns of signalling from the pathways involved, which can ultimately leave those regions under development from reduced input. The brain of a child, who is raped, for example, may react by reducing the connectivity of the regions that were hurt."[40]

PTSD is common amongst soldiers who return from war. Many experience haunting nightmares, distress, flashbacks, memory and concentration difficulties, and feelings of numbness. These effects can last for a period of days, weeks, or even years. Like physical scars that damage tissues, in some cases causing keloids to appear, depending on the skin type and its sensitivity, so it is with emotional scars that can affect the brain like keloids. These scars filter deep into the subconscious, preventing many people from passing over this threshold. These people become fearful and constantly feel ashamed, slipping in and out of depression. Their pain and the ensuing scars determine how they speak and live out the quality of their lives.

You and Your Emotions

Many people experience prototypical expressions, expressing themselves as life throws different punches at them. Some days they are sad, other days, glad, happy, angry, fearful, apathetic, shameful, proud, elated. These

---

[40] Szalavitz, Maia, and Maia Szalavitz. "Sexual and Emotional Abuse Scar the Brain in Specific Ways | TIME.com." Time. Time. Web. 28 Jan. 2015.

different kinds of expressions have a lot to do with your personality. If you are melancholic, you will express your anger in a different manner than a choleric, sanguine, or phlegmatic person might. All of these distinctive feelings and thoughts are usually expressed as what we refer to as emotions.

Our emotions derive from our state of mind. We were all born with them. Without emotions we could not know or understand people's feelings. In fact, it is said that one is emotionally intelligent when he has the ability to control and express his emotions, and is able to interpret others' emotions. Emotion is a feeling that is first processed though our brains. The brain tells us that something is affecting us, which then causes us to express an emotion. Our emotions influence our behaviour, our belief system, our social life, our intentions, and our actions. People have tried to repress, ventilate, and process their emotions in various ways. How people interpret what is happening to them in life contributes to their emotional well-being. The Bible tells us that we were made in the image and likeness of God. And it is clear that God has emotions—love, anger, regret—therefore, we were meant to have emotions also.

Managing Emotions

How we manage and process our emotions has a lot to do with our health. Our emotions can contribute to the physical illnesses we develop because our brains release different hormones based on our feelings. We are bombarded with a host of issues each day that can cause a build-up of negative emotions. An introvert processes her emotions differently from an extrovert. One will suppress their feelings, while the other will most likely express their feelings, regardless of their surroundings.

Let's look at the case of a child that has been repeatedly sexually molested or raped by a parent. How does this child process her unexplained and mixed feelings of love and hate? Not knowing what to do with the pain, this child bottles up her feelings of hurt and anger on the inside. She eventually enters into a relationship as an adult, and brings forth a child. Unfortunately, her offspring ends up living in fear because Mom has not healed and so is filled with anger and pain. As a result, Mom constantly hurts her child physically, verbally, and emotionally because of her unprocessed and unhealed emotions. Her child may eventually grow up with what is called inherited childhood pain, and she may eventually pass down this emotional pain to her own child.

Sometimes when people are afraid of dealing with their pain and shame, they repress their emotions by overeating, becoming addicted to using illegal substances, or engaging in other forms of compulsive behaviours. This leads to fatigue, depression, lack of social interaction, and isolation, just to name a few.

Let us look at some the negative emotions that arise as a result of unhealed wounds.

Depression

Depression is a state in which one is overcome by grief and sadness. This, of course, affects the other emotional aspects of one's life deeply and sometimes filters throughout different regions of the body, causing illness. The longer the depression lasts, the more pervasive it becomes. People get depressed for various reasons.

Sometimes traumatic experiences cause a chemical imbalance within the body, resulting in depression. The toxicity of one's environment can also contribute to depression. These experiences seep into one's thoughts, building a level of toxins which, over time, build up and poison that person's system, physically and psychological.

Untreated depression has shackled many and holds them in bondage. A depressed person sometimes struggles with confusion, not being able to understand their feelings or put the pieces together. One of the major issues that depressed individuals have to face is a low serotonin level. There are blood tests that measure the level of the serotonin deficiency and the treatment needed.

Depression can affect the overall quality of one's life. It has been known to change sleeping patterns, resulting in nightmares, insomnia, or a lack of deep REM sleep. One suffering from depression may also experience feelings of sadness, lack of interest in education, socializing, work, and family.

Grief

Grief and grieving is a form of emotional suffering that many humans experience at some point in their lifetime. It is a natural response to loss, and the process may be short-lived or continuous, depending on the reason for the grief.

Sometimes, when one's trust is violated, especially by one who should protect and care for you, there is a feeling of grief that results. This grief can manifest as an intense emotional pain accompanied by sickness, exhaustion, anger, or anxiety. This mixture of emotions can also cause a level of confusion that leaves you not knowing how to explain your inner pain.

Some common causes for grief include:

a) The loss of parent, child, spouse, or significant relationship

b) Being and/or feeling rejected or abandoned

c) The loss of one's innocence

d) The loss/lack of childhood experiences

e) The loss of trust and hope

f) The loss of control

Shame

Shame is a difficult emotion to deal with. In fact, many people have difficulty dealing with their shame after exposing themselves to individuals who blame them for what they've gone through. People who are critical and judgemental can be toxic, and are not the best people to help persons who are dealing with shame. Shame causes people to feel worthless, like they are never good enough.

Shame needs to be healed, so the best thing is to seek support from trusted individuals who can help to bring healing. Shame causes low self-worth. In fact, victims often want to hide or feel like walking with their heads hanging down because of their feelings of embarrassment and unworthiness.

Anger

Maya Angelou once said, "Bitterness is like cancer. It

eats upon the host. But anger is like fire. It burns it all clean". Everyone experiences anger at some point in their lifetime. Anger is usually accompanied by displeasure or annoyance. Anger can build over time, especially if a person has not been given the opportunity to face the source of their anger or see justice done. As anger builds, it has the potential of developing into rage—an extreme or volatile outburst of anger.

We must ensure that our anger does not affect those around us. This is a hard thing to do, especially when the anger we feel is a direct result of being violated, abused, neglected, rejected, or betrayed. The Bible teaches that we should be angry without sinning, and we should deal with our anger as quickly as possible.[41] When anger is released positively, it can leave a person feeling mentally liberated, meaning that the mind is free to think clearly and move on to the process of healing and forgiveness.

In his book, Christian Counselling Dr. Gary Collins points out that there are different types of anger as shown in the following [42]:

> a) Shame-based Anger: people who handle their shame by getting angry at their accusers or those assumed to be accusers. This anger style requires counselling to help separate anger from shame.
>
> b) Moral Anger: manifests as righteous indignation in persons fighting for a cause. Sometimes, this leads to violence and insensitivity. Help people channel

---

[41] Ephesians 4:26

[42] Collins, Gary R. Christian Counseling: A Comprehensive Guide. Waco, Tex.: Word, 1980. 165. Print.

this anger into more useful directions.

c) Depressive Anger: repressed anger usually reappears as depression. This kind of anger has the appearance of empathy, which leads to caring and reducing the sense of moral superiority. Treatment for depressive anger is two-fold: first treat the depression and then help the sufferer come to terms with the source of the anger.

Oozing Wounds

A physical wound is an injury to the body that results in a break in the skin or damage to bodily tissues or organs. Depending on the force of contact, a wound can be severe or minor and, depending on its degree, it may require special medical attention to prevent it from evolving into a more serious condition.

Physical injuries are not always avoidable and, especially in the lives of young children, they are often a part of everyday life. They teach us the consequences of certain actions, and they also educate us in the body's capacity to heal itself when tended to in a timely fashion. Some wounds can be fixed with a Band-Aid and a kiss, while others need the attention and skill of a medical professional. When tended properly, wounds heal over a period of time, but often leave a scar, a reminder of what happened. Though the wound was painful when it was raw and bloody, as time goes on, there only remains the memory of the hurt, and not the hurt itself.

Some wounds seem minor, and as such they are left untreated, and it is not until those wounds come in contact with another force that the true impact of the wound is realized. Case in point, a friend of mine bumped her hand on a wall, right between her ring finger and her pinky. She felt a bit of tingling in the area, but because it was such a small, random act, she didn't think much of the incident. It wasn't until she tried to use a pair of scissors with her hand a few days later that she realized that the two fingers had become swollen and could not move. It was four weeks before her injured fingers recovered their full range of motion.

Emotional wounds are similar to these 'minor wounds' in the sense that they are usually not acknowledged until a secondary traumatic trigger is encountered. Harsh, degrading words or an act of abuse can cause painful memories to flood the victim's mind, eliciting feelings of fearfulness, hopelessness, and worthlessness. The trauma of the wound then repeats itself in the mind of the victim, causing post-traumatic stress to manifest.

The Effects of Negative Emotions

As I stated earlier, our emotions control the way we think and behave. Therefore, negative emotions can limit our quality of life. They affect the way we communicate with others, our relationships, and our energy levels. A scenario was drawn by one of my counselling professors of two individuals who were tired—one went home and went to sleep, while the other went to church, regardless of feeling tired. The one who went to church and actively participated in the worship released a hormone that causes the body to heal faster than the person who went home to rest. Once the body senses the release of certain feel-good hormones—serotonin and dopamine—it triggers a healthy emotion. In other words, worship is like a detoxifier for negative thoughts and emotions. The moment you come in contact with the Divine, healing is fostered. On the other hand, though the one who went home rested her body, she did not tap into the full healing possible.

Any form of prayer, meditation, and reading of the Holy Word of God will release healing because we come in contact with the Divine. Worship is a form of therapy. Note that the Bible focuses on the importance of the mind, for it is with the mind that we serve God. I have come to realize that the dominion that God has given us does not manifest as it should due to the quality of the emotions we produce. Sin is a negative influence. Man was not made to sin, that is why we produce negative emotions that break the body down and result in major episodes, like heart disease, anxiety, and other chronic diseases.

I suffer from high blood pressure because of an overwhelming negative experience I had. I did not know how to deal with it or how to release the negative emotions that resulted, so I repressed them daily. This put my health at risk. I remember crying until I had no more strength to cry. But one night, just as I was about to enter into my time of devotion, with tears in my eyes, I opened my Bible and Job 5:19 stood out to me as if it was highlighted and enlarged for me to read. It read, "He will rescue you in six troubles; in seven nothing that is evil [for you] will touch you."[43] That word spoke specifically to what I was experiencing. That night, I felt like all the built-up toxic emotions were just oozing out of me like a draining

---

[43] Amplified Bible

wound. I said a prayer and went to bed with the word in my heart. I slept well that night because I understood that what I was experiencing was a part of my destiny. I realized that I can't choose my destiny, and so I just have to follow in the path that God has already mapped out to take me into my purpose. When we understand that God is in control of the things we experience, we can better handle our emotions.

Negative emotions, if left unaddressed, can lead to suicide or self-destructive behaviours. The following are some of the negative emotions that we need to be aware of: hate, fear, covetousness, grudge, unforgiveness, jealousy, bitterness, sadness, resentment, hopelessness, destructive criticism, suspicion, rage, hostility, grief, malice, rejection, sorrow, frustration, confusion, hurt, loneliness, regret, shame, and anxiety. All these negative emotions disrupt our ability to function properly, to make wise decisions and practice sound judgement. They obstruct our belief system, which in turn affects our perceptions. They contribute to premature aging, premature death, and gradually break the body down. Have you ever wondered why some people never have anything good to say about others? That's because they carry some of these negative emotions that hinder them from being at peace with others and seeing the good in others.

Some of our experiences in life will cause us to experience negative emotions, but we have the choice not to allow these feelings to lay dormant within us, shape our behaviour, or bring us to an early grave.

Positive emotions act as boosters for all of the systems in the body, as well as the mind. When we experience joy, love, peace, contentment, respect, acceptance, encouragement, empowerment, trust, or courage, our bodies release pleasure chemicals that create inner tranquility.

There are several ways to alleviate negative emotions, such as eating the right kinds of food, getting proper rest, exercising regularly, going to the spa or getting a massage, reading inspirational literature, meditating on good things, and even going on vacation. Positive emotions improve one's self-esteem, quality of life, and mental alertness, while reducing anxiety, mood swings, and stress. When we are aware of what negative thoughts and emotions do to our bodies, we will be more diligent in protecting our minds.

We must intentionally ask ourselves each day if our thoughts are appropriate. Examine your chain of thoughts. Whenever someone speaks negative things about you, choose not to respond negatively, rather force yourself to think positively. Remember that you are what you think. The Bible encourages us to cultivate the mind of Christ within us. Paul also tells us to arrest and take these negative thoughts captive.

Negative emotions are like congealed saturated fat or jelly; in that, instead of your energy flowing positively, it is blocked, so that you cannot move forward. When our energy is blocked, we remain stuck in our pain, stuck in transition, stuck with a false identity and false perceptions. Our negative energy leaves stains on our lives that are hard to remove. Toxic thoughts release toxic chemicals that alter the brain and emotions. They induce stress, and stress poisons the body internally until it manifests itself externally. As such, negative thoughts become strongholds that can only be broken and uprooted by the regenerating power of God. The seeds sown in our thoughts become a harvest of strongholds that affect every area of our lives. For this reason, we have to fight to maintain positive thoughts that contribute to positive energy.

Chapter

The Nature of the Christian Conversion

The Bible declares that God established boundaries in the beginning by telling Adam where he could eat and where he could not. The serpent, being beguiling, was able to tempt the woman to cross over the line of demarcation that God had set. Adam and Eve made a choice, and the choice was to disobey God. In so doing, there was a separation in the relationship and fellowship that they enjoyed with their Creator. Another result of their disobedience was the fate that befell all mankind from thenceforth—death. But thanks be to God that in the beginning, before all things were created, the Word of God, Jesus Christ, existed. John 1 declares that the Word was with God, and the Word was God Himself. All things were made by Him. And without Him nothing was made. In Him was life and His life was the light of men.

The world came into existence by the power of God's Word, which expresses the very image, character, mind, and attributes of God. That same Word manifested

Himself in the flesh; He became flesh and dwelt among us. This Word is the sole expression and the visible perfect imprint of the image of the Lord God Almighty.[44] It is this same Jesus that paid the price for our redemption and has redeemed us with His precious blood.

As believers in the death, burial, and resurrection of Christ Jesus, we have received our conversion by repenting of our sins and accepting the new birth of Salvation. We then become baptized in His name and receive the baptism of the Holy Ghost, which enables us to walk in newness of life.

What is Conversion?

In the natural sense, conversion is the turning away from one idea to accept a new and different way. It involves a mental persuasion that the way one has chosen is the better way. Spiritually, conversion is regeneration through faith by the blood of the lamb. It is the turning away from the ways of the world and accepting God. Just like Paul on the highway to Damascus, in order to be converted it is necessary to turn away from the path one is presently travelling on and turn to Jesus who is the Light of the world. Conversion involves a process of spiritual healing. Sin originates in the minds and hearts of people and only the powerful, efficacious blood of Jesus is able to cleanse and deliver us from this toxin. It is a change that must be voluntarily accepted, and its transformative process affects the entire man—thoughts, behaviours, motives, and feelings. It is an experience that goes beyond

---

[44] Hebrews 1:3

what any person can do for himself. After all, if we had the ability to spontaneously and immediately change our traits, we would! The power of conversion comes from accepting the sovereignty and omnipotence of God and surrendering ourselves to Him. As the Christian convert gives God the preeminence over his life, he opens himself to learn more and more about God and to witness Him at work. As the relationship between God and the convert develops, the convert becomes more pliable to the will of God, allowing Him to become like a lump of clay on a potter's wheel. As the believer yields to God's divine guidance, he will notice a change in his thought patterns, demeanour, and response to life's stressors.

Being Born Again

Nicodemus, a ruler of the Sanhedrin council, came to Jesus by night seeking the way to salvation. But what Jesus taught him was that salvation requires a sacrificial life.[45] The concept of salvation comes from the emancipation of Israel from slavery in Egypt, which is a symbol of our slavery to sin. God's plan of salvation is to deliver us from death by allowing us to be born of water, the Spirit, and the blood of Jesus Christ. This is evidenced in Acts 9, where Paul was knocked down by a bright light from Heaven. He, and those with him, heard a voice call out, "Saul, Saul, why do you persecute me?" When a person meets God, the spirit of knowledge that lies within has no choice but to acknowledge Him. Saul answered, "Who are you, Lord?" and the voice replied, "I am Jesus whom you

---

[45]John 3:1-14

persecute."

To give context to this text, Saul was a Jew who opposed the rise of Christianity, and was taking measures to arrest anyone caught professing the name of Jesus. In fact, prior to this event, Saul was inquiring of the high priest for the written authority to arrest any such persons. Yet, in the very act of going against God's will, Saul was stopped, heard the confession that Jesus is Lord, and had his mission redirected. What a conversion!

The Effects of Conversion

As we continue to look at the life of Apostle Paul, it is evident that through conversion God changed his human spirit. Conversion affects us holistically, and its effects can be felt spiritually, psychologically, and emotionally. It is clear that God cares about every intricate area of our being, and there is no part of us that God is not able to bring change, healing, and wholesomeness to.

Paul's conversion in Acts 9 changed his heart for the rest of his life. Paul emphatically stated that he was born out of an untimely birth. He was a persecutor and a murderer not worthy to be called an apostle of Jesus Christ. Paul's encounter was divine. He was never witnessed to by a human being, but God saw a man full of passion, zeal, and love for God who just needed to find the right way. Paul testified that he did not receive the gospel with any human aid, rather his transforming change was through the revelation of Jesus Christ, who enabled him through grace to preach the gospel to the gentiles.

During Paul's conversion, he became physically blind and had to be led by those who were with him. Though he lost his physical sight, he was given spiritual insight.

His eyes were open to the mystery of Jesus Christ. Both his perspective and his spiritual position changed. There was visible evidence that a change had taken place. When Saul came in contact with Jesus, others could perceive the difference. Paul's radical, anti-Jesus stance changed immediately.

Unaware of what was happening, Ananias, a disciple in Damascus, saw the Lord in a vision. In the vision, he was given directions to the place he should go to meet Saul. Upon hearing the name of the man he was to find, Ananias told the Lord that Saul's reputation within the Christian community had been widely discussed. He had heard of Saul's actions in Jerusalem towards the saints and how he had the authority of the chief priests to seize and arrest all who believed in Jesus. But God told Ananias to go nevertheless because Saul was His chosen vessel.

God can use anyone to fulfill His will. It is unlikely that any of us might have a past as dark as Saul's. Yet, when Ananias presented Saul's past before the Lord, the Lord's reply was simple, "Saul is now working for Me." Saul was not the only instrument used by God that had flaws. King David, Rahab, and Apostle Peter are just a few other examples. Therefore, it is a clear fact that when a man or woman meets God, the conversion is life-altering.

Conversion Changes the Way We Think

"Let the wicked forsake his way, and the unrighteous man his thoughts: and let him return unto the Lord, and he will have mercy upon him; and to our God, for he will

---

[46] Isaiah 55:7

abundantly pardon."[46]

Our thoughts are influenced daily by the culture and environment we live in. Hence, in order for the Holy Ghost to channel Himself through us, our thoughts must be renewed. Just as new wine cannot be stored in old bottles lest the wine break the bottle, so we cannot have positive thoughts until we get rid of the toxic, negative thoughts that imprison us. In James 3:11, the Bible tells us that a fountain cannot send forth bitter and sweet water at the same time. Something has to give way. Likewise, we must make the conscious decision to change. Each individual must first recognize the need for change and pursue that transformation with his whole heart. Our spirit, mind, and emotions are intertwined by divine design. That is why when the spirit of a man is wounded, it affects him psychologically, emotionally, and physically.

I believe that spirituality plays a role in our psychology. In 2 Corinthians 10:5, Paul tells us that we must bring into captivity every thought to the obedience of Christ. He also tells us to gird up the loins of our minds. In other words, don't just allow your mind to run wild by thinking all manner of thoughts. Instead, we must discipline ourselves and take control of our thoughts and be mature in our thinking. It is a fact that our thoughts determine our outcome.

Conversion wires us for greatness and helps us to attain the highest version of ourselves.

Chapter 7

Redefining Your True Self

It is important to keep in mind that our environment has a lot to do with our lifestyle. The word environment refers to our surroundings, where we spend our time. Your personal environment includes where you go to school, your community, where you work, where you worship, and, most importantly, where you live. Every environment has a social influence and has the ability to shape our identity. Your environment contributes to various aspects of your life, whether positively or negatively. It can either make you or break you.

A person's identity can be viewed as multidimensional. We all have a personal identity, a social identity, a legal identity, a religious identity, a cultural identity, and probably several other forms of identity. In his book, Discovering the Eagle Within, Dr. Clarence Duff states that "many social psychologists believe that the image we have of ourselves is at least partly derived from the people with whom we associate. The people who formed part of our social lives at different stages of our development usually leave significant impressions on our sense of self."[47]

In order to redefine yourself, you must completely let go of your past—the name calling, the accusations, the failures, and the mistakes. You are a survivor of a painful past, and now it is time to move forward. Jesus has given us the key to unlock every chain. He has given us the key to break the invisible chain of bondage, the chains that have imprisoned us for years, the chains of shame and fear. I believe that God has given us all that we need to live a successful life, but we tend to search for validation in others, rather than in what God has already given us. Therefore, to redefine yourself, you must begin to see yourself in the light of God's word. To move forward, you must take the journey in your subconscious and 'scroll and delete' the hidden negative thoughts, words, and feelings. If you don't, these feelings will reappear and hinder your progress. This process may not be a big leap, but rather a series of baby steps forward, until you gain the strength and courage to leap.

It is an unfortunate fact that children who have been abandoned by parents may not have felt the parental love that serves as a foundation for their ability to express and experience love. It is not uncommon for these individuals to find it very difficult to receive love. This process may

---

[47] Duff, Clarence. Discovering the Eagle Within: A Guide to Understanding Your Inner World of Potential And... S.l.: Word Alive, 2013. 59.

then involve opening up, receiving love from others, and regaining trust.

Shakespeare once said, "To thine own self be true." Redefining yourself means letting go of toxic people, toxic environments, and toxic past memories. It means discovering the authentic you that lies beneath a life filled with pain. There is greatness beneath your shame and fear. There is a beauty that you mask each day—your sense of humour, your loving nature, your understanding heart. You are not a victim, and you are not just a survivor, you are more than a conqueror.

In 2 Corinthians 12:9 Paul said, "But He said to me, My grace is enough for you; for *My* strength *and* power are made perfect *and show themselves most effective* in weakness. Therefore, I will all the more gladly glory in my weaknesses *and* infirmities, that the strength *and* power of Christ may rest upon me!" Stare weakness, brokenness, scars, wounds, and failure in the face and triumph over them. Redefine yourself and your broken pieces will come together. In Jeremiah 18:6, God took Jeremiah down to the potter's house and asked the question, "Oh house of Israel why can't I do to you as the potter does with the clay?" God specializes in mending broken vessels. You can't be too broken for God to mend you and put you back together. He has the power to do the impossible.

As you take this journey of transformation, just like the eagle that picks out her old feathers to grow new ones, the process can be painful. Yet, to be whole again, God must get rid of all your cracks. He desires to give you total healing. Only the potter's touch can mend you. He can restore your shattered life and heal your hidden pain. His tender touch can mould you and fold you on

His potter's wheel. He can saturate you with His healing water, and transform your brokenness into a vessel of honour to bring glory to his excellent name. His wooden mallet will remove all the air bubbles, those pockets of unseen faults and failures that can cause your vessel to crack and break. His firing process will bring a structural change in your life, making you firm and durable enough to carry His glory and His anointing without leaking it. He can make you pliable and useable for His purpose for your life.

In the movie *The Wizard of Oz,* the two characters that stood out to me the most were the Tin Man and the Cowardly Lion. The Tin Man wanted a heart, and the Cowardly Lion wanted courage. Courage is needed to overcome situations that are dangerous or threatening in any way. Both the Cowardly Lion and the Tin Man were looking for character traits that they already had, they just needed to discover them. Likewise, God has already deposited the seeds of potential within us from before we were born. Therefore, we do not need to go searching to for new traits, we just need to accept the tests that God sends our way to prove to us what we have on the inside.

It's not your past that defines you; it's the power of your thoughts. Death and life are in the power of the tongue. You can change your life by the thoughts you think and the words you speak. It's your thoughts that determine your success. People's definitions and labels do not dictate your future. Everyone has a past, but not everyone allows their past to define their ability to succeed. You can be great regardless of the "nobody" your past had labelled you to be.

I encourage you to purpose in your mind to start

redefining your life, starting today. Start to journal your success, goals, dreams, and vision as you see it in the future. Write down those realistic goals and pursue and recover all that the enemy has taken from you. Focus on being successful, and success will knock on your door. You must bring your mind, body, and spirit to the level where healing will take place. If you are still bitter, this process could take longer. But once you get to the right level, healing will take place.

Redefining Yourself Through Prayer

1 John 5:14-15 says, "This is the confidence we have in approaching God: that if we ask anything according to his will, he hears us. And if we know that he hears us—whatever we ask—we know that we have what we asked of him." And Jeremiah 33:3 says, "Call to me and I will answer you and tell you great and unsearchable things you do not know."

Prayer is a powerful explosive. It is the basis of an intimate relationship with God. We pray because we have confidence in the Word of God that He is faithful, just, and righteous to both hear and respond.[48] Believing God's Word reinforces our faith and confidence in Him that He will deliver, heal, and establish our steps. Jesus has given us access to the throne room. His Word is the key we use to access His immediate presence, and prayer is the weapon we use to tear down, build up, root up, and plant according to God's divine will. Matthew 7:7 tells us to ask, and it shall be given to us; seek, and we will find; knock,

---

[48] Hebrews 11:6

and the door will be opened for us.

Does your situation seem impossible? Prayer connects and fuses us with the eternal God. Prayer is like a safe haven where we can unload from the storms of life. It is a method whereby we can be refreshed, and restored. Life can throw some terrible punches sometimes, but in 1 Chronicles 4:9-10, we read about Jabez, who was described as being more honourable than his brethren. Yet, his mother named him 'sorrow.' Jabez called on God and said, "Oh, that you would bless me and enlarge my territory! Let your hand be with me, and keep me from harm so that I will be free from pain." And in the end, God granted him his request.

One of the busiest shopping plazas in Canada, Toronto's Eaton Centre, was named after Timothy Eaton, founder of the Eaton shopping chain. He did not come from a wealthy family; rather, he was the child of Irish immigrants. As a young man, he opened a small shop in rural Ontario in the 1860s, which went bankrupt within a few months. In spite of this setback, he continued forward with his entrepreneurial dreams and opened another store not long after. With this new venture, he started new initiatives—sending catalogues to neighbouring towns to promote his store and his merchandise as well as offering customer satisfaction or a refund. These were new for the 1860s consumer, but Eaton was determined to succeed. Just like Timothy Eaton, don't allow past failures to define your ability to achieve future success. Even worse, do not allow others to throw cold water on your future. You can be great regardless of your past.

Redefining yourself starts with examining yourself to see the God-given ability and potential that God has placed within you. Let's look at a courageous woman mentioned in 2 Samuel 21. This woman was dauntless, determined, loyal, and faithful in death. She was a woman who showed stamina, not only as a mother but also as an advocate for her children. She was the daughter of Aiah, and the mother of Armoni and Mephibosheth, she was King Saul's concubine, whom Abner later took as a wife, and her name is Rizpah. Her two sons were put to death on account of Saul's actions. However, Rizpah was loyal to her sons, even in their death. She positioned herself on a stone which could easily symbolize her strength and confidence. She was firm in fighting for what was right. This woman took her sackcloth and spread it out upon the rock from the beginning of harvest, which is in the month of April, until the beginning of the rainy season, which is in the fall. Let's picture this passionate, courageous woman sitting there for six months, protecting the dead bodies of her sons from scavengers and wild beasts. Picture her there in the rain, the sun, and the lonely nights, driving away the vultures from her sons' bodies. As the days went by, their bodies began to decay and become stink. This situation must have been unbearable, but Rizpah was determined that her sons would not be eaten by vultures or wild beasts. She was probably exhausted, hungry, and hot, but she was determined to stay on guard. Due to the fact that these boys were King Saul's sons, they deserved a proper burial. As such, this woman was an activist for her sons.

King David heard of Rizpah's loyalty and how she fought for justice and a proper burial for her boys. His compassion reached out to her, and he granted her request. Rizpah was indeed a hero.

Your Past Has No Power Over Your Future

Regardless of the psychological and physical torture you have endured, it has no power over your future. You have the ability to build and step into your future. Your faith in God gives you the resilience to push forward. Life teaches us that when we experience the bitterness of life, we should push and move forward into a new pathway.

In childhood and adulthood, we will experience life's punches, but how we deal with these experiences will depend on our faith, resilience, biological genetics, and our environment. We cannot tie our present or even our future identity to our painful past. You are not your past. You are not a failure. Once you plug into Jesus, the True Vine, the Word of God, He will light your pathway.

In the time of the judges, there was a famine in Bethlehem-Judah. Elimelech took his wife, Naomi, and left for Moab. While in Moab, their two sons married two of the daughters from Moab, Ruth and Orpah. As the years went by, Elimelech and the two sons died. After living in loneliness, word came to Naomi that the famine was over in Bethlehem-Judah. Naomi felt that there was no need to stay in Moab, so she made the decision to return to her homeland. Naomi's two daughters-in-law travelled with her a short distance, until Naomi told them to stay in Moab. Orpah took the advice of her mother-in-law and returned to her parents. Ruth, however, knew her past was buried with her father-in-law and her husband back in Moab and that her future was with her mother-in-law. When Naomi begged Ruth to return, Ruth boldly declared that she would let go of her past and hold on to her future. As Ruth released her past and embraced her future, she was fulfilling a role predestined by God. Moab meant deadness for her and she had intended to embrace life by leaving the past. What incredible faith.

Ruth, the Moabitess, converted to Judaism through her remarkable commitment to her mother-in-law. Ruth spoke prophetically over her own life when she renounced her county, her people and her gods to accept Naomi, her country, people and her God. Although Ruth came from an idolatrous nation that served Chemosh and practiced child sacrifice, she inherited a great legacy and was placed in the lineage of the great Messiah. If God has a plan for your life, He will use any means to get you out of your old life and into the life He had preplanned. Ruth and Naomi entered Bethlehem during the barley harvest, a time of gathering food to store up for the winter months ahead. After settling in, Ruth volunteered to contribute to the household by gleaning in the field. Israelite law gave provisions for the community to provide for the poor. While gleaning, Ruth happened to glean in the field of Boaz, a near relative of Elimelech, Naomi's deceased husband. The Bible records that Boaz said to his servant, "Who is that damsel?" Ruth had caught the attention of Boaz. This tells me that though she had left her past behind, she did not look distressed. By the second chapter of the Book of Ruth, we notice that favour was upon Ruth. Boaz instructed the men to favour Ruth. Boaz also encouraged Ruth not to leave his field, but rather to stay in his field and glean. Her past was not a hindrance to her future, for she consciously made the decision to leave the past behind.

This story shows us that we cannot allow our pain to deform our true identity. Ruth's loyalty, faithfulness, and kindness brought her to the king's table and to the lineage of the greatest King ever to walk this earth—Jesus the Messiah. What a remarkable story of a young woman who was willing to leave her pain and grief behind and embrace an unknown future. Because of her denouncing her god, she is celebrated today in the Jewish and Christian communities. She is a model of a true survivor. She left the worst behind her and believed that her best years were ahead.

The time is now to let go of your regrets, rejection, pain, hurt, disappointment, shattered dreams and broken heart. Let it go! Lot's wife could not leave her past, Sodom had owned her. She was trapped in her past. She could not move forward, she looked back in remorse while leaving Sodom, and became a pillar of salt as a result. Refuse to allow your past to cause you to become a pillar of salt. Make that decision, like Ruth, to denounce the past. Acknowledge the effect your past has had on you, empty yourself of the bitterness, unforgiveness, and grudges, and claim the things that God has in store for you. Jeremiah 29:11 tells us that His thoughts towards us are thoughts of good and not of evil, to give us a hopeful end.

God can use your bad experiences to change a nation. Your negative experiences can turn into a positive future. You have the tenacity and the resilience to run through a troop and leap over a wall. You do not have to identify with your painful past. Your early development does not have the final word over your life. The Word of God has that final say. The Word of God can change the chemistry of your brain. God's Word is potent and efficacious to deliver us. Look at your negative past as one that sets the foundation for your future, like a stepping stone. I'm reminded of a story I was told as a child. A man's donkey fell into a hole so deep that no one knew he was there. The hole was used to dump garbage. In order to survive, the donkey had to eat the garbage. What he didn't eat, he used to form stairs to get out of the hole. The moral of the story is that sometimes we have to do what the donkey did. The garbage that is thrown on top of us to destroy us can be used to help us get to where we want to go.

God has often used the negative to create the positive. Consider a young lady who was constantly raped, starting at the age of seven. Her mother had different partners over the years and two of those men crossed the line that should exist between children and adults. After trying to tell her mother about the verbal and physical abuse she had endured, this woman lived a lifestyle based on her past. Her self-image was shattered. She lost hold of her identity and allowed people's perception of who she was to shape her life. This young lady told me that she kept a diary of all the things that were done to her in her past. I tried to encourage her to let go of those things, to forgive, and to move on from a past that was affecting her health and eating habits. I encouraged her to burn every bit of her journal.

Can You Burn Your Journal?

For some people, writing down their feelings in a journal can be a form of release, a way of expressing themselves. Yet, this young lady confessed that each time she revisited her journal, it would bring back the pain of the abuse as though it just happened yesterday. I wanted to tell this young girl that I also had to burn my journal. I had to free myself from the burden of my past, empty myself of the emotional pain, and release myself into the new world that God had ordained for me. While journaling can be very therapeutic, when we use it as a dumping ground for our thoughts and emotions, it can cause the negative feelings to fester, never allowing us to truly disassociate from our pain. I encourage you to do yourself a favour by burning your journal or anything that binds you to your past. Burning your past is called Restorative Therapy. As you burn these items, you begin to feel free. The load seems to fall off, and the constrictive shackles vanish, giving a physical and emotional feeling of freedom. This therapy brings healing to your life, both physically and psychologically. Facing the things you are afraid of and realizing that not everything that looks like a giant is a giant will help you to conquer your past.

We cannot fulfill our purpose until we make the conscious decision to change and transform into the true versions of ourselves. I encourage you to let go and allow yourself to become the true you. God has called us to be more than we think we are, and more than people have defined us to be. God has invested a wealth of resources in us that we can use to accomplish and become our higher and better selves.

Chapter

The Making of a New Mind

Do you want change? Renewing your mind involves changing your thinking, your expectations, your attitude, and your behaviour. When damaging thoughts have kept you bound to guilt and shame for years, they will undoubtedly have a harmful effect on your life in some way. A new way of thinking will produce a new way of living. In Romans 12:1-2, Paul entreats us not to conform to this world, but to be transformed by the renewing of our minds, so that we may prove the good and acceptable and perfect will of God. Creating a new mind can be a painful process because of the level of change one must go through.

Genesis 37 tells us that Joseph was his father's favourite child, and his brothers took note and were determined to get rid of Joseph. They sold him to the Midianites, who in turn sold him to Potiphar. Potiphar's wife concocted a lie against him, which caused Joseph to end up in prison. But while he was in prison, God was with

Joseph, building and making a governor out of his life. The evil he experienced was working out for his good. He said of his brothers' actions that they meant it for evil, but God meant it for good. He was a renewed man, even though he experienced abuse, betrayal, rejection, and hurt. This man had a change of mind and he began to view things from God's viewpoint. His thoughts had been completely renewed.

Our perceptions govern our behaviour. How we think affects the social, spiritual, and mental aspects of our lives and has the ability to distort our purpose. A thought can be very powerful. During the creation of the world, God's thoughts manifested, and everything was created. The thoughts of God created humanity. God then gave us freewill, which empowers us to choose and become what we think. Our thoughts determine who we are and what we will become; they will either make us successful or unsuccessful.

There are times when we abuse ourselves with our own thought patterns. The job of the enemy is to destroy us by infiltrating our minds with negative, oppressive thoughts. I believe that not only do drugs and other chemicals affect the brain, but the psycho-toxic thoughts we allow to linger can also change our brain's chemistry. These psycho-toxic thoughts shape your character, guide your integrity, and tend to control your destiny. The word psycho-toxic means "having or being a detrimental effect on one's mind, personality or behaviour."[49] If left

---

[49] Psychotoxic. Merriam-Webster. http://www.merriam-webster.com/medical/psychotoxic. 28 Feb. 2015.

unaddressed, these psycho-toxic thoughts soon begin to control and dominate your being. Thoughts of fear, anxiety, bitterness, and low self-worth are impure and poisonous ideas that enter the bloodstream and flow through the various systems of the body, causing decay. These sickly thoughts can affect the nervous system and other systems of the body, resulting in several kinds of diseases, including high blood pressure, diabetes, and depression. They age the individual by causing wrinkles, age spots, and other age-related symptoms. But just as drugs affect the brain and other aspect of the body, and in order to recover from the effect of the substance and the damages it has done, one has to be rehabilitated and detoxified. We must weed out all the bad seeds that the enemy has planted and get rid of the negative thoughts.

Psycho-toxic thoughts cannot live anywhere else but in an environment that is conducive to them, in an environment that feeds and nurtures them. God has given us freewill and the right to be in control of our thoughts and minds. We have the ability and the authority over ourselves to bring down every thought that depresses and oppresses. We have the will to choose and to control what comes in and out of our minds.

Mental Scars

Scars can be permanent, causing PTSD and severe damages to one's sense of self. These scars are constant reminders of the pain you experienced. Hence, each day you see the scars, they reduce your self-concept, especially when they are scars of emotional and verbal abuse. Scars like "You are dumb, stupid, fat, ugly," or "You have ADHD." These are labels that leave scars of your self-concept.

Many who have experienced childhood trauma tend to battle with midlife crises, all because of the long-lasting scars that won't go away. These scars stigmatize, disfigure, discolour, and leave blemishes that may contribute to changes in the chemistry of the brain. Rose Kennedy said, "It has been said, 'time heals all wounds.' I do not agree. The wounds remain. In time, the mind, protecting its sanity, covers them with scar tissue and the pain lessens. But, it is never gone." The same way the brain has built in receptors for some substances, I believe there are receptors for the negative thoughts we harbour. Sometimes, thoughts can become addictive thoughts to the point where they become strongholds.

Moving Towards Total Healing

Jeremiah 29:11 reminds us that God's thoughts towards us are thoughts of good and not of evil. We can make a conscious decision to move from powerlessness to being powerful, just by taking back our power. We can choose to be victors and not victims. We can refuse to become our story. We can let it go, be proactive, and empower ourselves with the Word of God. Yes, they threw Nelson Mandela in prison for twenty-seven years, yet Mandela made the right choice to let go of the pain and forgive his offenders.

Forgiveness comes when you identify and release your pent up emotions of anger and hurt. It must be done out of free will. Forgiveness does not mean that you have to reconcile with the people who intended to take your life or to harm you. Forgiveness is not so much for the abuser as it is for the abused. When you have come to terms with what was done to you, you have to decide whether you're going to stay in the cage and die or get out and live. You are the only person who can release yourself from that cage. The moment you get to the place where you begin to pull inner strength from God, and decide to change your thinking, you are free. Yes, I know there's a battlefield going on in your mind, I've been there myself. But I got to the place where I purposed in my heart that this battle would be won, and I would come out of my cage a winner. I may come out limping, but I was coming out an overcomer. Many years may have been wasted in the prison of past hurt, but you have the power to take off those chains and release yourself from those shackles. Life is precious, so it's time to change those negative years into positive, successful years. Yes, change is possible. You may find that it is not an easy task, but with the help of therapy and the guidance of a counsellor or psychologist, along with Jesus's skillful healing hands, change is possible.

There is a little quote at the Women's College Hospital in the mental health department that says, "You cannot hurt me anymore." This quote indicates that we have the power to control and govern our lives and protect ourselves from any form of abuse. It's time to take back your power and go after the healthy lifestyle you've always dreamt of. It's your time to live life to the fullest. You hold the power in your hands to change your world. Free yourself from guilt, self-blame, and shame.

You can be made whole. You can be loosed by the power of Jesus's precious blood. A new day has dawned, and it is time to touch the hem of Jesus's garment; you shall be made whole. You will indeed experience moments of confusion, fear, and distrust, but use all these unhealthy emotions as stepping stones to a brighter future. When he was being chased by King Saul, who sought to take his life, David encouraged himself in the Lord. He became retrospective and displayed confidence in God.

Forgiveness

Paul Boese once said, "Forgiveness does not change the past, but it does enlarge the future." I know what it's like to have difficulty forgiving those who hurt you to the core of your being. But not forgiving is a weight and burden that is too much for anyone to bear. The worst thing you could do with your life is to become stuck in unforgiveness. Forgiveness is not condoning the wrong an individual has done to you, but rather it's aligning yourself with the will of God. Hence, I do not believe there is such a thing as premature forgiveness.

Forgiveness is for you, not your offender. Are you finding it difficult to forgive those who have scarred you? Start by focusing on yourself and your own healing. When you can forgive yourself for errors you made in the past, you can find the measure of forgiveness you need to release to those who hurt you. Drop the charges against your offender, and remove the sting of vengeance you carry around on the inside. We cannot wait until people feel accountable for the wrong they have done because some people will never embrace that. Bring healing and inner peace to yourself by letting go of resentment, revenge, bitterness, anger, and negative thoughts. Forgiveness leads to future glory. Your empowerment is in the gift you release to yourself. Your whole life depends on your choice to forgive.

Spiritual Implications of Forgiveness

The benefits of forgiveness are inner joy, peace, health, and healthy relationships. It liberates you and connects you to God. What does the Bible say about forgiveness? Peter thought he had it all figured out when he boldly asked Jesus how many times he should forgive his brother. Jesus replied seventy times seven.[50] The Bible also tells us to forgive and we shall be forgiven by the Father.

It is not true forgiveness if after we pardon our offender we continue to seek revenge against that individual. The Bible clearly tells us to leave all vengeance to God.[51] And if you sit waiting for vengeance to be executed on that person, Proverbs 24:17-18 tells us that we may end up reaping the opposite. In other words, when you sit and wait for something bad to happen to another person, even the individual who wronged you, God will take note of the condition of your heart and God may withhold His punishment from that person.

The Bible says that our prayers are hindered when unforgiveness blocks our communication with God. On the other hand, forgiveness liberates and empowers us to work in our calling. It is a faith walk.

Martin Luther King, Jr. said, "He who is devoid of the power to forgive, is devoid of the power to love."

---

[50] Matthew 18:22
[51] Deuteronomy 32:35

The Power of Pardon

Nelson Mandela, a hero and an icon, has shown us that forgiveness makes you powerful. It shows a person's strength and, today, Mandela is viewed as a "towering figure of forgiveness." Forgiveness opens doors of opportunity and releases mega life. It is the key to future glory.

Your past may seem like a horror story. Maybe you were neglected, abandoned, and rejected by your parents, then when you thought life would get better, you were sent to a foster home, only to realize that your new parents were addicted to alcohol and drugs. And each time they got high, they would abuse you. This was the story of a young girl I spoke to once. As she told her story, I fought to hold back my tears because I could feel her pain. Another young girl I spoke to was constantly beaten, threatened, and raped by her stepfather. As she cried, she felt the weight of the bitterness she had been carrying for years. She felt as if she had no capacity to forgive. Unforgiveness painted her as a stone-faced victim—hard and callous.

People from all walks of life experience hurt, pain, troubled times, and trauma of every sort. And not once would I try to minimize anyone's pain, but we can move beyond our past. It's not an easy situation to handle, especially when you can still hear the abuser's voice in your head like a demon echoing abusive words. But we have the Word of God as our compass, reminding us that we are defined by God only and nothing else.

Unforgiveness does not heal us; it only allows the pain to live longer. The part of your life that was badly hurt is only a part of your life. You have the potential to make the rest of your life productive. You were born to succeed, so the pit you were thrown in is not the end of your life. The fact that you are still alive and breathing tells that there is more for you to fulfill.

To pardon means to acquit someone of the wrong they have done. Just as Jesus has extended mercy and grace to you, He has made it possible for you to also pardon others. Forgiveness changes your paradigm. It changes your thinking, your heart, and your physical health. Have you ever seen a bitter and unforgiving person whose posture has changed on account of bitterness? Forgiveness brings positive energy back into our lives and revives us.

When Jesus forgave this world, He released the power of forgiveness us, enabling us to let go of any hurt and pain that held us bound. When Jesus Christ declared "It is finished!" He was indicating to the world that that which He had come to do was now done. The spirit and power of forgiveness was made available to all through the work of the Cross.

You have the potential to forgive. Yes, forgiveness is possible when we reflect on the fact that we were first forgiven by Christ. Matthew 6:14-15 states that if we forgive others when they sin against us, our Heavenly Father will also forgive us. But, if we do not forgive, then our sins will not be forgiven. Jesus knew that we all would encounter some form of hurt, pain, or disappointment at the hands of others. That is why He enabled us to release the power of forgiveness that lies within us.

Chapter

From Deliverance to True Healing

Wounds that are not properly dealt with will not properly heal. It is like a child who has a serious cut on her finger, yet refuses to let you touch it, or even worse, clean the wound. Though the body has the natural ability to heal itself under the proper conditions, there are steps that need to be taken to ensure that wounds heal properly and without any complications. Likewise, emotional hurts cannot heal if they are not addressed in the right way.

I once lived the life of a child who was victimized, and I have learned that whether an abuser is a family member, a close family friend, or a total stranger, victims of abuse carry hurts and pain far longer than the duration of the incident. Though the wounds may have dried up and are no longer bleeding, just below the surface there is still unhealed tissue that stings. But thank God there is hope.

I thank God for the blood of Jesus Christ and the Body of Christ. Jesus is the greatest psychiatrist, counsellor, and therapist one could ever find. For many of you, your pain is hidden, and you fail to communicate it to anyone. But hidden pain is like skeletons in the closet and, after a while, it will be discovered regardless of how well you attempt to hide and protect it. Your wounds won't heal if they have not been dealt with. Expose your scars. Your scars are your stars. Your future depends on the care you give to your scars.

Oprah Winfrey and many others who have encountered abusive situations, now enjoy a glorious life that cannot be compared to the evil they suffered, all because they decided to let go of their past and move into their true destiny. You too can turn your negative experience into something positive, not just for yourself, but for the generations to come.

Today, because I allowed God to bring wholeness and healing to my emotions, I can reach out to people who have encountered various hurtful circumstances and help to prevent these experiences from happening again. I believe there is hope for every individual out there. You have to program your mind to feel hope and walk in that hope. In Job 14:14, Job asked the question, "If a man dies, shall he live again?" The answer is "Yes!" Friend, Christ is the Living Water that can bring you back to life. I believe that your future is more glorious than your past.

The Process of Change

We sometimes experience things in life that cause us to desire change. However, change can only happen when we have purposed in our hearts to change. Change must be sought; it must come from a desire that is propelled by purpose and destiny. Change can be a painful process to undergo, but it is necessary. Without change in our lives, we are hindered from progress and greatness. When we are able to flush the negative things out of our minds, and reprogram our thoughts, we will be able to take positive action by carrying out the things we desire to change in our lives.

In order to facilitate healing in our lives, we must be able to recollect the broken areas that the enemy has disfigured, and come face to face with the little child inside of us that has endured much pain. Change is possible when we come to grips with our past. Change is possible when we acknowledge our condition and accept what happened, rather than disown the realities of what caused the blockage in the first place.

Change will come when you purpose in your mind that you will embrace the pain and conquer the hold it has on your life. Change will occur when you have a plan of action. Change will occur when you enter into a relationship with Christ and bring that wounded inner child into His presence and allow him to heal that pain wholesomely.

I remember going to a retreat as a young girl, feeling heavyladen and burdened by past hurt and rejection. As I began to pray and cry to God, a voice spoke to me in a comforting manner. And as I gave God my emotions, I began to feel His divine hands of healing on my life. I can testify to you that prayer works. Jesus is the only one whose words can heal, cleanse, and deliver at the same time. His words are the most powerful words any human being can ever experience. His voice will calm the soul, stop the bleeding, heal the wounds, and remove the scars. His is the only voice that is powerful enough to eliminate verbal abuse, rejuvenate the soul, and demodulate every past trauma and pain. He will even reprogramme your memory from past marital or childhood abandonment or rejection.

Change is possible when we acknowledge the self-inflicted pain and self-blame we have carried for years. Change is possible when we sense that urge to become the person God wants us to be. Change is possible when we begin to see deeper meaning to life; when we become aware of our purpose and desire to walk in that God-given purpose for our lives. Change is possible when we purpose in our hearts to forgive those that despitefully used us. When we purpose in our hearts to release bitterness, hate, and resentfulness, and fill the void with the love of God and His peace.

Transition

Transition moves us from a state of comfort to a place of confusion, discouragement, and being overwhelmed. Transition is the act of changing from one state to another. It is a process of change that can sometimes cause uncertainty.

Let's look at the butterfly's and the eagle's transition process. The butterfly changes from an egg to what is called a larva or caterpillar. Then it changes from a caterpillar to a pupa, and finally from a pupa to a butterfly. During this process of change, the butterfly experiences a lot of pain, but it must change completely in order to become a beautiful butterfly.

The Hebrew word for eagle is nesher, which means to tear with the beak. The eagle is the king of all other birds. He is a brave and fierce fighter, and is often used to symbolize strength and beauty. The eagle goes through a molting season, which causes moments of depression and agony. There is a calcium deposit that accumulates on the talons and the beak, and in order to get rid of this calcium deposit he has to beat those areas against the rocks. This is a very painful process. Through this process the eagle becomes weak and loses his strength. At the same time, he is shedding his old feathers by pulling them out and making space for new feathers to grow.

Isaiah 40:31 speaks of God renewing our strength and causing us to soar with wings like an eagle. Many birds seek for refuge when the forecast indicates that there will be a storm, but the eagle is not afraid of the storm. Instead, he rides out the storm by focussing on the eye of the storm.

I believe that just as the eagle was built with the mechanism to withstand the storm, so are we built to withstand the storms of life. God has given us the skills to endure and embrace the thunders and lightning of life. This is why the Bible declares in Isaiah 43:2 that when we pass through the waters, God will be with us. What a consolation to know that the eternal God watches over us and will be with us in the midst of life's storms.

Life comes with different categories of storms—job loss, loss of a loved one, unemployment, sickness and diseases, accidents, catastrophes of every kind, loneliness, rejection, and abuse. It is sometimes very difficult to see God while in the midst of the storm. When when we keep the mindset that Jesus is with us, we will not be overthrown by the storms.

Jesus also experienced a transitional period. Jesus endured the cross as they pierced him and mocked him.

He laid down His life to give us life, then three days later, He arose from the grave. He took the keys of death and hell, and declared to Heaven and earth that all power is given unto Him.

We live in a changing world where everything around us goes through transitional change. Every day we are bombarded with hundreds of thoughts that change our perspectives. We experience daily environmental change, social change, physical change, and spiritual change, so start believing that you are capable of changing for the better.

Change is the result of moving to the next chapter in your life. To initiate change, you must first acknowledge the need for change. You must also prepare yourself for change by preparing your mind. This transition requires a lot of self-talk. Bring forth all the positive within you, and affirm yourself as you begin to change your core belief system.

Take control and stay away from negative actions that can cause relapse. There is always a positive side to changing, even though the process can create fear and anxiety. The process of change allows you to shift into your highest self and see yourself in a clearer light. This process is continuous and involves organizing certain steps that need to be taken, and setting goals that you want to achieve at the end of the process.

We have the ability to change because we have power over our thinking. This power allows us to change our thoughts, our perceptions, our emotions, and our behaviours. This kind of change is not always easy, but we can achieve anything we put our minds to accomplish. Keep in mind that this kind of change will also change our health for the better.

So, are you ready for a change?

My goal is to help you change how you see your experience, how you see yourself, and how you associate with your past. It can be a battle to remain positive when you're in a toxic environment, surrounded by toxic people. It is a battle because you have to fight to protect yourself, your mind, your body, and your spirit. If you are not careful, their negativity can seep into you. Some of the ways to maintain your positive thoughts are:

- Monitor your thoughts
- Monitor your feelings
- Monitor your behaviour
- Monitor your words
- Don't overgeneralize your experiences
- Don't focus on negative experiences
- Focus on positive experiences

"What am I gaining from all this?" you might ask. The answer is a better you, a better quality of life, peace of mind, and clearer lenses to view the world. Keeping track of your thoughts and emotions for one to two hours per day will gradually help you to maintain a healthy thought pattern.

Avoid Toxic Behaviour

Toxic relationships and toxic behaviours can destroy your self-image and your dreams if you allow them. Toxic people usually undermine your values. They are usually controlling, manipulative, and tend to want to govern your life. Being exposed to toxic people or toxic environments will contribute to an unhealthy life, since they can act as triggers that cause you to relapse.

A toxic person's goal is to make sure you are unhappy. Despite what that individual might have done to you, he or she always portrays themselves as the victim. Toxic people believe they are always right. They usually use their power to abuse you verbally and emotionally. These kinds of people create high stress and contribute to many of the health issues you may face.

Toxic people can be found in the workplace, in church, in your community, and everywhere else in society. Therefore, you have to take the initiative to prevent them from having power over you. They cannot let you do anything you don't want to do. They may influence you, but you have the power over your own life. Don't dance to their music or eat of their lies. These people are usually attention seekers. They have emotional issues, but always point their fingers at others to imply that it is others who have the issues.

Regardless of the picture they paint of you, always have a sound and positive mindset, stay focused, and refuse to be a reflection of their toxic behaviour. Because they're so toxic, they will intoxicate you if you are not careful. Toxic people intoxicate others, so if you have to spend time around these types of people, then be sure to detox your mind and spirit once you leave.

Taking Care of You

Every now and then I visit the wellness centre for

a holistic approach to my wellness. I go through what is called a deep tissue body massage, total lymphatic drainage, hot rocks on my back, and a reflexology massage of my foot and hands. This therapeutic session brings me renewed energy, removes blockage, eliminates emotional, mental, and physical toxins, and enables me to have better spiritual focus. This process also helps me to relax in my everyday life and helps me to cope and handle social relationships better.

I was told that as we get older and less active, the lymphatic system slows down and tends to cause blockages, so having a lymphatic drainage helps to eliminate not just toxins, but also built-up protein and bacteria in the body. This was a very painful process for me, but my therapist reminded me that "no pain, no gain." While I was doing the lymphatic drainage, she asked me if I can tolerate the pain and I said that I would for a good result. Even though it hurt badly, I kept focusing on my health, not the pain. At one point, I felt like I could touch the roof, that's how intense the pain was. Then, I remembered how Jesus endured the cross, despite the shame. You see, Jesus was focused on doing the father's will. Likewise, we have to focus on our goal, and not on the pain. The therapist then recommended that I go into the sauna afterwards to alleviate the pain and help eliminate the toxins that were released during the draining process. I highly recommend this process to anyone who wants to maintain a healthy lifestyle, especially after experiencing traumatic events.

Draining Emotional Wounds

Being in the healthcare field, I happened to come

across a patient who had surgery and had to have what is called a wound drainage chamber connected to her. This is done when the doctor suspects infection or bacteria around the operating site. Patients tend to carry symptoms like pus and fluid around the wound, accompanied by pain, swelling, and redness. When I saw this situation, I thought of draining emotional wounds in order to foster and speed up the process of healing. This drainage chamber also enabled the doctor to detect bacteria, germs, and viruses.

Emotional drainage is similar, except in this case the process involves venting, releasing fear, anger, distress, built up tears, detoxing the conscious and subconscious mind, and purifying the emotions. During this process, it is important to always focus on your goals with the intent of recovering yourself.

This process is not for everyone. Some people tend to cope with trauma better than others; we are all different. Some will allow the trauma to submerge into their subconscious mind and be locked away and buried for so many years that they become disassociated from the traumatic event, to the point where they are in denial.

I believe that if victims go through this process with a therapist or counsellor, they do not have to bring this traumatic pain into a new relationship. Many relationships are ruined because the other person cannot understand the victim's dysfunctional behaviour. Many spouses suffer on account of unresolved issues and the lack of healing in their partner's life. Are you suffering because a spouse has walked out on you and left you bleeding, confused, lonely, lost, angry, and ashamed? It's time to stop the hurting and heal the pain. Connect yourself to a support system like a church or trusted friends. Recover yourself after separation or divorce, and transition into your new life.

You don't need to feel lonely, depressed, unworthy, or unloved anymore. Thanks be to God, there is hope at the end of the tunnel. As you take this journey to not just being delivered from the situation that has haunted you for years, but being truly healed, God's strength will undergird you. Your complete healing awaits you.

Chapter
10

From Deliverance to True Healing

Isaiah 43:19 declares, "I will do a new thing in you." How can an ordinary life become extraordinary? Through faith in God and believing that He is well able to do exceeding abundantly above all that we can ask or think. God is willing to see past your pain and lift you above your past. If you can push past the traumatic pain you are encountering or have encountered, then you can redefine your life through personal development.

There is a level of greatness that is on the inside of you, a great level of courage, strength, and tenacity that you have not yet utilized. Your extraordinary power was challenged by your abuser, but now it is time to make a comeback with excessive extraordinary power. Purposefully deepen your awareness of your authentic self, rediscover your God-given purpose in life, refine your character, recognize your potential, reclaim your life, take back your power, and soar like the eagle. It's only when you begin your journey of self-actualization that you will conquer self-oppression and self-doubt.

Are you hungry for change? Don't focus on the emotional pain; instead, focus on unleashing your inner power and energy, and releasing yourself from the past. Re-align yourself. Set realistic goals, and pursue vision and positive change that will foster and bring forth successful achievement. If you are weak in your mind, my suggestion is to change your environment and remove yourself from the negative people who will never see the good in you. The development of your new self depends on the kind of environment and friends you associate with. If your friends are not motivated or successful, then it may be hard for you to redefine yourself in their midst. Your environment can sometimes be filled with pressure, but when you are determined to possess what God has promised you, you will be free.

The Church in the Community

The last days are upon us, and many lives have been shattered and broken. The church is the only entity that is unbreakable and unshakable; it is the place of refuge that the world needs. The core purpose of the church is to facilitate, guide, and provide governmental order, to build up values and morality in communities, and to pull down immorality. The church is the lifeline of the world.

According to Jesus's teachings, the church's responsibilities include evangelizing the world, making disciples out of men and women, and loving our neighbours as ourselves. We are the light and salt of the world. Therefore, every church program, policy, and procedure must, and should, incorporate the community. It's time to throw out the lifeline into the community and rescue the lonely, the oppressed, and the physically challenged. Yes, I said the physically challenged because there is a place in the church not just for able bodies, but also for those held back due to disabilities.

The church is supposed to be a hospital that is filled with social support for every aspect of the human encounter. The church is filled with people with healing hands for the emotional, physiological, and spiritual well being of the total person. The church has the capacity to nurture, support, heal, build, strengthen, and comfort the individual. It is the responsibility of the church to be a buffer that protects the people of God from any threatening danger.

People cannot find peace and live morally upstanding lives without the aid of the church. We have a mandate to cater to the needs of the community in a holistic manner. In fact, Ephesians 4:10-16 tells us that God gave various gifts to the church to build up and edify the world. Therefore, it is your job and mine to do our part in helping those who are suffering to experience true healing through Christ Jesus.

Conclusion

The battle for the mind is intensified each day, but regardless of how intense the battle gets, we must be determined to win the war.

The fact is that abuse in any form is wrong and should not be tolerated, regardless of who the abuser is. But be reminded that negative emotions will imprison us; and, like poison, the longer they linger the worse they get.

However, the Christian conversion changes things by bringing about a change of mind and heart. God helps us, through Christ, to see the big picture in life. He also helps us to face our pain and climb over it into new life.

In closing, I urge you to redefine yourself, and take the step to move from deliverance to the path of true healing. In Christ all things are possible.

Appendix

Value I Cherished

A confidence was instilled in me at an early age by my teacher, Mrs. Henry. She was a very outstanding person, well dressed, well spoken, and when she walked, she walked with one of the most beautiful postures I have ever seen. She was a teacher that we, the young girls at Bethany Primary School, admired.

This lady came into my life at a very crucial time— just when my mother migrated to Canada to give us a better life. Mrs. Henry was a good friend, and became like a mother to me. She believed in the children in her class and loved each and every one of us as if we were her own children.

As I recall, my school was on a hill and my physical education class was always in a valley. I remember coming from that class one day, and because I was so weary from running a race, I walked with my legs wide apart to make it up the hill. Mrs. Henry saw me and said that she didn't want any of her young girls to walk like that. I can remember from that day onward that she taught and groomed all of us in how we should conduct ourselves as young ladies.

Today, most of us who were in her class walk with our shoulders back and our tummies tucked in. This lesson has shaped us to walk in confidence, believing in ourselves. She taught us how to love, and how to be kind and compassionate. Those were values instilled within me that caused me to become resilient. Because of her lessons, whenever I am hit down by challenges and traumatic experiences in life, I know that I will bounce back and accomplish my dreams. I have learned to keep my head above the waters, to never to give up, regardless of the spin the wheels of life may take. These values, along with my Christian values, became the core values that kept me afloat during the storms of life.

The Creaking of the Door

Winter in the tropics was the feeling of each night. Stiff and pale as a ghost, cold as a popsicle, wrapped in blankets from head to toe. Fear gripped my heart like a racing horse. Could this be happening again? "Oh, God!" I cried. "Where are you?"

My cover is gone, my beauty, my power, and confidence, wrapped in shame, stooped in a corner in fear and trembling.

Who am I?

I've lost my identity.

Who am I?

Does anyone care?

As I gazed in the mirror, I became pale.

Lonely eyes filled with pain and fear. "Oh, God," I cried, "let him stop. Keep him away from me!"

Does anyone even care? Has God abandoned me? Fear grips my heart. Oh no, can I live with God?

Silently, I cried for months.

I have lost it all, my dignity, my pride, my values, my integrity, my joy.

"Oh, God," I cried, "restore me."

As I yearn for those precious moments, moments of innocence like Alice in Wonderland. Depression eats at my emotions; pain, shame, and fear are my friends. Will I ever be happy again?

I wish I could feel the arms of Mom around me. Mom, where are you? I desperately need to feel love and care.

Then I felt the warmth of loving arms around me. I felt calm, I felt peace, I felt renewed, I felt clean. Oh, God, it must be you. Yesterday I cried painful tears.

The storm is gone. The cold has passed. Out of my shell, out of my sorrow, out of my darkness and shame. I have found refuge under His wings.

One hot summer day, like the song says, "Baby, we found love right where we are." Handsome, dark, and tall, eyes sparkling glitters like gold—dancing eyes, eyes filled with hope and love. He was all I wanted, and one day he took me down the aisle. I wore his ring. He is mine.

As the years went by, his life became a fragmented puzzle with pieces I could not find to put together. His dancing, glittering eyes became filled with silent pain, pain he never disclosed, hidden scars of childhood pain.

He wore the mask for years. He was sensitive, argumentative, and agitated.

"Oh, God," I cried. "My love, my darling, his life is filled with silent pain."

Could it be that the man I married was abused as a child? Traumatized? His friends are but few, they never come around. His relationships are unsound.

"Lord, it's me again."

This time his healing hands were eminent. My tears were gone, my peace restored.

My forgiveness is for all of you, but most of all it's for me. Forgiveness is freeing me from the pain and agony, freeing me to live a life of peace and freedom. I am free, free at last.

Bibliography

Collins, Gary R. Christian Counselling. Rev. and Expanded ed. Vol. 3rd. Milton Keynes: Word, 1989. Print.

Connelly, Elizabeth Russell. Child Abuse and Neglect: Examining the Psychological Components. Philadelphia: Chelsea House, 2000. Print.

Duff, Clarence. Discovering the Eagle Within: A Guide to Understanding Your Inner World of Potential And Thoughts. S.l.: Word Alive, 2013. Print.

Duff, Clarence. Unlocking the Mystery of Depression: A Psycho-theological Exploration on How It Happens, How It Is Prevented, and How It Is Healed. Belleville, Ont.: Essence Pub., 2003. Print.

Iverson, Timothy J. Child Abuse and Neglect: An Information and Reference Guide. New York: Garland Pub., 1990. Print.

Leaf, Caroline. Who Switched off My Brain?: Controlling Toxic Thoughts and Emotions. New ed. S.l.: Inprov, 2009. Print.

Radbill, Samuel X., and C. Henry Kempe. A History of Child Abuse and Infanticide. Chicago, Ill.: U of Chicago, 1968. Print.

Online Resources

"BibleGateway." .com: A Searchable Online Bible in over 100 Versions and 50 Languages. www.biblegateway.org.

Cherry, Kendra. "Nature vs Nurture: Do Genes Or Environment Matter More?" http://psychology.about.com/od/nindex/g/nature-nurture.htm.

Encyclopedia Britannica Online. Encyclopedia Britannica. www.britannica.com.

"Facts on Child Abuse and Neglect - Canadian Red Cross." Red Cross Canada. Web.

Healy, Melissa. "Heartache or Headache, Pain Process Is Similar, Studies Find." Los Angeles Times. Los Angeles Times, 4 Apr. 2011.

Merriam-Webster. Merriam-Webster. www.merriam-webster.com.

"One-third of Canadians Have Suffered Child Abuse, Highest Rates in the Western Provinces, Study Says." National Post Onethird of Canadians Have Suffered Child Abuse Highest Rates in the Western Provinces Studysays Comments. Web.

"Psychology Today.": Health, Help, Happiness Find a

Therapist. https://www.psychologytoday.com.

"S.W.I.R.L | The Five Stages of Abandonment | Susan Anderson | Abandonment Recovery." Abandonmentnet RSS. Web.

Szalavitz, Maia, and Maia Szalavitz. "Sexual and Emotional Abuse Scar the Brain in Specific Ways | TIME.com." Time. Time. Web. 28 Jan. 2015. .

The Free Dictionary by Farlex. http://www.thefreedictionary.com/black+sheep. 15 March 2015.

Wikipedia. Wikimedia Foundation. www.wikipedia.org

About the Author

Marcia Dixon-Haye studied at George Brown College and is presently doing a degree in Christian Counselling and Theology. She works at Sunnybrook Hospital in clinical pathology. She is also an ordained evangelist at Bethlehem United Church. Marcia frequently works in the community as a motivational speaker and retreat trooper.

Marcia currently lives in Brampton, Ontario with her husband, Lee-Roy, and her two children, Anthony and Kenesha.

www.ingramcontent.com/pod-product-compliance
Lightning Source LLC
Chambersburg PA
CBHW070157100426
42743CB00013B/2951